PRAYING

for Those with

ADDICTIONS

A Mission of Love, Mercy, and Hope

ANNE COSTA

the WORD
among us®
Press

To my friend Kathy

"Faithful friends are a sure refuge:
whoever finds one has found a treasure."
(Sirach 6:14)

Published by The Word Among Us Press
7115 Guilford Drive
Frederick, Maryland 21704

20 19 18 17 16   1 2 3 4 5

ISBN: 978-1-59325-295-3
eISBN: 978-1-59325-485-8

Cover design by Coronation Media

Made and printed in the United States of America

Library of Congress Control Number: 2016941500

Contents

Introduction / 6

1. God, Where Are You? / 16

2. Hitting the Wall / 30

3. The Courage to Change / 43

4. Searching for Clarity / 54

5. One Day at a Time / 63

6. The Remedy of Joy / 76

7. The Pathway to Peace / 86

8. The Truth Shall Set You Free / 101

9. Praying with the Saints / 115

10. Letting Go / 127

11. Keeping the Faith / 138

12. Passing It On / 146

Prayers / 155

Resources / 164

Bibliography / 169

Notes / 170

Introduction

This book is written to offer hope in the hell storm of addiction. It will set you on course for a mission of love and mercy and for a miracle of healing, not just for the person who is addicted, but for yourself as well. If you purchased this book, it is because you probably already know too well how desperately help and healing are needed in the face of any addiction.

The statistics are grim. It is estimated that approximately 53 percent of Americans have one or more close relatives who have an alcohol dependency problem. In addition, 43 percent of American adults have been exposed to the problem of alcoholism in their family, either as something they grew up with or something they experienced with a spouse or a partner, and 6.6 million children under the age of eighteen live with a parent who struggles with alcoholism.[1] According to one poll, 47 percent of families in the US reported that pornography is a problem in their home.[2] An estimated 6 percent of American college students struggles with gambling problem, and as many as 750,000 young people ages fourteen to twenty-one have a gambling addiction.[3] There is also an estimated 9 million prescription drug abusers in the US,[4] along with a growing epidemic of opioid addiction. To sum it up, 63 percent of Americans are affected by addiction, either by their own addiction or that of a family member.[5] I suspect that the percentage is actually much higher.

While these numbers represent the cold hard facts of addiction in our country, they can't speak to the countless broken hearts and lives that are affected. For we know that it is not just the addicted who suffer but all those who love and care for them—family, friends, and co-workers alike. Chances are that there is not a single person among us who has not in some way been touched by addiction.

Addiction of any sort is a very personal condition. Experts tend to study it in terms of a general disease process and to apply evidence-based scientific interventions to develop treatment options. However, how addiction affects each individual's mind, body, and spirit or why people become addicted in the first place is due to a complex and individualized set of factors that we are still only on the brink of understanding. As a result, there is no single solution or approach to treating or curing addictions.

What seems clear is that at the heart of every addiction is a wound that needs to be healed. While many have found that the support and fellowship offered through a twelve-step program seem to have the longest-lasting effects, we don't really know how or why they work for some and not for others. *What we DO know and can believe is that prayer works and faith fixes things!* We know that God ministers to the brokenhearted:

> The righteous cry out, the LORD hears
>   and he rescues them from all their afflictions.
> The LORD is close to the brokenhearted,
>   saves those whose spirit is crushed. (Psalm 34:18-19)

We can stand in the gap through prayer, sacrifice, and supplication for the one who is addicted. Our prayers can, and will, make a difference. As we are encouraged by Scripture,

Is anyone among you sick? . . . The prayer of faith will save the sick person, and the Lord will raise him up. . . . Pray for one another, that you may be healed. The fervent prayer of a righteous person is very powerful. (James 5:14-16)

How We Pray

The *Catechism of the Catholic Church* describes three expressions of prayer: vocal prayer, meditation, and contemplative prayer.

Vocal prayer "associates the body with the interior prayer of the heart, following Christ's example of praying to his Father and teaching the Our Father to his disciples" (CCC, 2722). It is the spoken words of our hearts when we cry out, offer thanks, or pray a novena or special intercessory prayer to a saint. Vocal prayers are like the four walls of our prayer closet. They are the foundation and pillars that make it possible for us to go deeper into the interior room of our souls as we approach God with our needs, desires, joys, and sorrows. Vocal prayers are just the beginning of our conversation with God.

Meditation "is a prayerful quest engaging thought, imagination, emotion, and desire" (CCC, 2723). Christian meditation leads us into a discernment of God's will and teaches us how to pay attention to the life of the Spirit within us. One of the most popular forms of meditative prayer is the Rosary. It combines vocal prayer with an invitation to reflect on the life of Jesus as we pray through the beads.

Another effective means of meditation is through a process known as *lectio divina*, which means "divine reading" or "sacred reading." It is a method of reading a short passage or verse from Scripture in a slow, deliberate, and repetitive manner (usually three separate times) while listening for a word or impression that speaks to our hearts. We reflect on that word or impression and ask the Holy Spirit to reveal its significance to us personally. *Lectio divina* will often lead us to insights that we can apply to our daily lives in a practical and helpful way.

Contemplation, in the words of St. Teresa of Avila, is "taking time frequently to be alone with him who we know loves us" (CCC, 2709). Characteristics of contemplative prayer are silence, intensity, and a gaze of faith that is fixed on Jesus. The outcome of contemplative prayer is union and communion with Christ and an increase of love in our hearts. Going to adoration and simply receiving what Jesus wants to give us, as well as gazing upon a crucifix with love, are examples of contemplative prayer.

St. Paul urged his friend Timothy "that supplications, prayers, petitions, and thanksgivings be offered for everyone . . . that we may lead a quiet and tranquil life in all devotion and dignity" (1 Timothy 2:1-2).

Not a single prayer goes unheard in heaven. When we pray for others, we are making a difference in a very real way, both spiritually and temporally, in our own lives and in the lives of others. Even when we don't know what or how to pray, Jesus is continually offering up prayers for us through his Holy Spirit: "In the same way, the Spirit too comes to the aid of our weakness; for we do not know how to pray as we ought, but the Spirit itself intercedes with inexpressible groanings" (Romans 8:26).

When we take up the mission to pray for those who are addicted, our prayers become an ongoing dialogue that saves, heals, and leads us and our loved ones and friends who are addicted back to the heart of the Father and the freedom he alone can give.

Prayer is powerful, and it works!

My Story

Although I have no professional credentials in the field of addictions, I have a lifetime of experience dealing with them. In fact, both of my parents were what we refer to today as "adult children of alcoholics." Together they carried the burdens, shame, and scars from their own childhoods into their new family unit and simply did the best they could. Without really understanding why or how, they played out what they had always known—they became alcoholics themselves, living a life fraught with the chaos, silent rage, pain, and crippling effects of alcoholism and codependency.

As their only child, I learned, as if by osmosis, how to make the necessary adjustments in the struggle to survive. I focused all my energy and attention on how to keep my parents from drinking because when they did, life got very scary and unpredictable. So I walked on eggshells, trying to be perfect and pretending that everything was normal even when I felt completely abnormal and out of control on the inside.

By the time I was a teenager, I was so riddled with anxiety and depression that I was willing to try anything to make life better, including taking in the very substance that was causing all the pain in the first place: alcohol. By the age of eighteen, I was a full-blown alcoholic. For ten years, from my last year in high school until my first year of marriage, I spiraled down into the bottom of a bottle. Alcooholism clouded my judgment, impaired my growth, made me sick, left me wallowing in shame and self-loathing, inflamed my fears, and crippled my soul; and no matter how many times I vowed to quit, I couldn't.

You are probably wondering, "So how did you get from there to here?" If you are reading this book, I am certain that you have a high stake in the answer. You might be desperately seeking to figure out what you can do to help your loved one quit the behavior that is slowly killing his or her soul. Maybe you have neglected yourself and your own life in the process. Maybe you have set some limits, only to have them violated time and time again, leaving you bewildered and ashamed. It could be that you have let go of your last shred of hope or are filled with a fury that threatens any semblance of sanity or peace in your own soul. Or maybe you are just profoundly sad, and sick and tired of being sick and tired of loving or caring about someone who is addicted.

What I have learned on my own journey is that we serve a God of infinite mercy, and his heart especially overflows with love and a desire to free those imprisoned by addiction. In fact, the one person who seeks restoration even more than you do for your friend or loved one is Jesus. He came to set the captives free, and there is nothing more binding than an out-of-control addiction (or even a seemingly under-control one) that slowly robs someone of their very essence.

I've also discovered and have come to believe that every addict is confronted by grace on a daily basis but may be too soul-sick to notice. I believe that there is not just one moment of spiritual clarity but many that are offered by the Holy Spirit to get the attention of the person caught in addiction.

In fact, there may be many "rock bottoms" made available until an addict hits the one that sets him on the road to healing and recovery. And the same is true for every person who loves an addict.

That's because you have the potential to be just as soul-sick with worry and preoccupation as the addict you love. You could be living an out-of-control life as well, or one of quiet desperation. You may have set your very self aside in order to rescue, save, hide, control, or otherwise manipulate or mitigate the damage that the addict has done or is still doing in his or her own life, your life, and the lives of others. This is a full-time job, and *it isn't yours*. It falls under the occupational title of "Impossible," and the only one who has the qualifications for that job is God.

As a friend or co-worker or concerned neighbor, you may be a bit more removed but saddened nonetheless. Standing by as someone spirals down into an addiction can leave one feeling helpless, confused, or cut off. Maybe you don't even know the person who is addicted, but someone has asked you to pray on their behalf. For all of these circumstances and more, this book is written to bring encouragement, strength, and hope in the midst of the pain and sorrow of addiction.

Certainly the fact that I am writing this book is itself a miracle. I have been sober (by the grace of God) for close to twenty-seven years. I still remember that one profound moment of clarity back in November 1989 when I finally grabbed hold of the hand of grace that was reaching down from heaven to pull me out of the pit and into the freedom that Jesus had died to give me. It was a quiet moment of decision made in the depth of my broken heart.

I am convinced that the only way that I was able to hear
that small voice of God amidst the screaming terror of my
addiction was because someone, somewhere, was praying for
me. Prayers are the best weapons against addiction. And spe-
cific prayers prayed in repetition, like novenas (nine successive
days of prayer) or the Rosary, can release spiritual strongholds
and break generational patterns and bondages that result in
addictions.

Please don't think that I am taking anything away from the
personal responsibility of the person who is addicted. Each one
of us has the best gift that God could give us besides his Son,
and that is the gift of our free will. There will always come a
time when a person with an addiction will have to exercise
his or her will in the form of a personal decision to quit the
addiction once and for all.

It is a decision that can't be arranged or forced by anyone
else. It is as much a mystery as any other action of God in a
soul. As friends and loved ones who are the bystanders to the
three-alarm emergency of addiction before us, we can simply
pave the way to that decision with our prayers. It is our way
of cooperating with God's grace. It is our mission of mercy
and love.

How to Use This Book

It is my hope that this book, when used as a guide for prayer
and self-reflection, will have a deep impact on your life and the
life of your loved one or friend with an addiction. My prayer
is that with each page, you will sense the Holy Spirit's invitation to greater understanding, consolation, and healing.

I have arranged the content and prayers in such a way as to enable you to use this book on a prayer journey for an entire year if you so choose. The first section is made up of twelve chapters, one for each month. Each chapter contains four sections that can be read throughout the month or from week to week. At the end of each chapter, there are four Scripture verses that correspond with each week in the month. You can claim each Scripture verse and pray or meditate upon each one daily (as in *lectio divina*). There is a reflective question to go along with each verse to spark your meditation or to write about in a prayer journal.

Two simple prayers will be included for you to pray each week—one for your own growth in the Lord and one interceding for the person who is addicted—for a total of ninety-six short vocal prayers in all. Sometimes we don't know how to pray, and sometimes we can't. These prayers are included here to give you a place to start. If something springs to your heart and mind as you pray, there is also space for you to write your own "Heart Prayer" at the end of each chapter.

A second section of the book is made up of longer prayers and novenas to patron saints and contains prayers for special circumstances. There is also a link to an online special "Prayer of Blessing," which is a formal blessing that is intended to strengthen the addicted person in the struggle to overcome addiction and also to assist his or her family and friends. Also included is a list of some helpful resources.

A final thought before you begin: keep things as simple as possible. Try not to get hung up on the form of how to use this book. Take what you need and leave the rest behind. There is no right or wrong way to pray.

I started this book by telling you that I am here to offer hope. The Scriptures tell us that it is "in hope we were saved" (Romans 8:24). And Jesus said, "Therefore I tell you, all that you ask for in prayer, believe that you will receive it and it shall be yours" (Mark 11:24). Believe that when we unselfishly offer heartfelt prayers of intercession for others who are addicted, we are helping them in the very best way we can, and that in the process, we are helping ourselves too. For as we pray for others, we, too, are being healed. No matter how we pray, Jesus hears our prayers, and he will answer them in his own time and in his own way. His love is stronger than any addiction—on that we can depend.

CHAPTER ONE

God, Where Are You?

God, grant me the serenity to
accept the things I cannot change,
courage to change the things that should be changed,
and the wisdom to know the difference.

L et these first three lines of the original Serenity Prayer by
Rev. Reinhold Niebuhr be our foundation as we embark on
our prayer mission for our loved ones who are addicted.
They are a guide for us as much as they are for those who are
addicted, and will lead us into a deeper understanding of the
way we should go on this journey.

A friend once described the experience of loving someone
who is addicted as trying to harness a hurricane. In the midst
of all the chaos, worry, and pain, we can get tossed about, and
God can seem so very far away. Yet in reality, God is not far
from us but very, very near. As Scripture points out, God has
the power to calm the storm of any addiction:

> They reeled, staggered like drunkards;
> their skill was of no avail.
> In their distress they cried to the LORD,
> who brought them out of their peril;
> He hushed the storm to silence,
> the waves of the sea were stilled.
> They rejoiced that the sea grew calm,

that God brought them to the harbor they longed for."
(Psalm 107:27-30)

I am inviting you to believe and cling to the hope that God can and will calm the storm in your own life that has been caused by the addiction of someone near to you. Even if right now you feel no sense of hope, claim his grace to bring about the serenity, courage, and wisdom you need to carry out this prayerful mission.

Claiming the Grace

How do you claim God's grace in the midst of turmoil and confusion? The short answer is through the intention of your will. What that means is that your feelings, your questions, and your deep desire for a swift and painless release for your loved one from addiction all have to play "second fiddle" to your desire for God's grace and presence to enter in your midst and the situation right now, with things just as they are. Sometimes we become so focused on the way we wish or want things to be that we miss the grace that God wants to infuse into our lives and plant in our hearts in each present moment. *It is a matter of intentionally claiming God's grace and accepting the consequences!*
The *Catechism of the Catholic Church* defines "grace" as "the free and undeserved help that God gives us to respond to his call to become children of God" (1996). We belong to him; through baptism we are his adopted sons and daughters, but he does not force a relationship upon us. In fact, as life goes on, we often collect many idols and allow many things

to take the primary place of God in our hearts. Sometimes we form attachments that can bring about darkness and lead to our own destruction. Addiction is just one outward manifestation of this vulnerability toward idolatry, or of putting people, places, or things before God in our lives and hearts.

Claiming God's grace means that as much as we are able, we turn our full attention back to the Lord. It means that we grab hold of grace as the lifeline that the Holy Spirit throws out to us so that we can fully participate in the life of God. But before we can grab hold of grace, we need to let go of our own preconceived notions of how we think things should be. This letting go is not a onetime event but an ongoing commitment to our own spiritual freedom and peace, one day at a time. It even means letting go of our loved ones into the loving embrace of our good God so that he can heal them from the inside out.

Essentially, addiction is a form of spiritual "heart dis-ease." If we get caught up in someone else's addiction, it has the potential to create a deep division and imbalance within us. We become disconnected from the core of our being, where God lives and moves and has his being and from where his grace, serenity, and wisdom flow.

When I first got sober, I had no recollection, understanding, or conscious experience of God's grace or serenity in my life. Even though I had been a Catholic all of my life and had loved Jesus very much as a child, the life I had been living and the bondage I had been in made it impossible for me, at first, to experience the spiritual part of my being. It was as if the Holy Spirit was buried and my faith locked up and frozen. It took several years for the Lord to thaw me out!

Throughout my healing journey, the Lord has had to patiently teach me all over again who he is and how to pray. It may be the same with your friend or loved one. Healing from an addiction on a spiritual level can take time. Recovery is so much more than the absence of the substance or activity that we know as the addiction.

What helped most in those early years of confusion and disconnectedness were my encounters with people who truly embraced and embodied serenity in their own lives. For me, they were like walking billboards of who I wanted to be—they had something I wanted. Through their witness, I was seeing a sign of the peace of God's grace.

Sometimes the addictions of those we know can bait us into reacting rather than responding with compassion. If we are dependent upon or in close relationship with someone who is addicted, we can especially fall prey to the temptation to try to control the person or the addiction. In the process, we can lose our own sense of peace and serenity.

As friends and loved ones of those who are addicted, realize that who you are and what you stand for will have much more influence and impact than what you say or don't say or what you do or don't do in your relationship. Recognize that when you stand firm in your belief and hope in a God who personally cares for each one of us and forgives us no matter what we've done, you offer a contrast to the hopelessness and despair that a person who is addicted experiences on a daily basis. Even though people who are addicted may cover up these vulnerable feelings with anger, negativity, indifference, or a false bravado, they hunger for hope and an authentic witness and the experience of God's saving grace.

Pour your energy into being an instrument of God's grace and a witness to his peace.

Accepting Reality

When my daughter was younger, she loved to go to the playground. Every week we would find a new one to explore. One afternoon we ventured out after a light summer rainstorm, and before I could warn her, she was up on the jungle gym. Within a few seconds, she slipped on a bar and tumbled to the ground.

As I ran to her, she jumped up, dusted herself off, and proclaimed, "I'm okay—it doesn't hurt!" But she didn't see what I saw, which was a deep gash above her eye that was starting to bleed and swell. "I'm alright!" she shouted in response to my badly concealed horrified face. "I just want to go back and play!" It wasn't long, though, before she started to feel the sting and the reality of what had just happened. Then as she fell into my arms, the tears came, and we headed off to the hospital for stitches.

This scenario reminds me of what it can be like when we are in a relationship with someone who is addicted. Sometimes instead of acknowledging our pain, we "keep calm and carry on"—to a fault. Denial is a big part of addiction, often even for those who are on "the outside looking in." Making excuses, covering up, minimizing our own pain and disappointment, and pretending it isn't there can all play a part in our own reaction and relationship to the person who is addicted.

How comforting it is to remember that our Jesus is always gentle with those who are troubled! His compassion and mercy are endless. Inviting the Holy Spirit, who is also known as the "Spirit of Truth," into our situation and the relationship with the person who is addicted will help us to see things as they truly are. This opens the door to God's powerful intercession. God can't heal our hurts until we acknowledge we have them.

Escaping from reality is exactly what every person who is addicted is trying to do when he or she becomes actively involved in an addiction. For example, it's easy to make the connection that people who are addicted to sex or pornography are often running from authentic intimacy. Other types of addiction may distance a person from his own moral core or his obligations to family, work, or community. The addiction process aids people in the pursuit of a state that resembles spiritual ecstasy but with the wrong "god." People caught up in addiction are seeking a holy union by unholy means! (That's why a spiritual program of recovery works so well, once they choose to embrace it.)

The late Catholic psychologist Fr. Adrian Van Kaam has noted that the addicted person is in perpetual pursuit of the substance or experience that will "take him out of the world of task and commitment."[6] This leaves those who love that person outside the realm of intimacy and interest, and accepting that reality can be very painful. Loving or being in a relationship of any kind with an addict, even from afar, can be a profoundly lonely and frustrating experience.

The closer the person is to you, the more painful and precarious life becomes, and there's no getting around it. Because addiction is a progressive disease, the longer it goes untreated, the greater the likelihood of suffering for all who are touched by it. Therefore, when we choose to stay connected to someone who is addicted, we need to learn good methods of self-care and preservation.

Taking Responsibility for Ourselves

Acknowledging our own need for love and respect can be difficult at times. When someone close to us is in the throes of an addiction, it is like living in the midst of a three-alarm fire. Oftentimes, we are on "high alert," trying to negotiate our way through the wreckage and get clear of the smoke that constantly obscures our view. The last thing we are thinking about as we try to save our loved ones from the disaster of an addiction is putting on the oxygen mask ourselves.

Yet just as we are instructed on an airplane to put on our own mask first, we need to attend to our own needs first in order to be of any help to someone else. We especially need to take care of ourselves when relationships are difficult and one-sided, as they often are when people are involved in active addictions.

You may have heard the phrase "You can't love anyone until you love yourself." But do you really believe it? Loving ourselves by taking care of our own needs is not selfish. It is honoring the God who lives and breathes and has his being within us. In fact, learning how to love ourselves is the means by which we come to know, accept, and receive God's love more fully. We love because he loves us first, and it is in discovering the depth of his love for us that we are able to love others as he does.

A wise person once remarked that victims are self-made. He was able to say that because he had spent a lot of years being a victim—a learned behavior. In his mind and through his actions, he was always expecting the worst while hoping, and sometimes even demanding, that others step up to the plate and make his life better. He was placing all of his hopes for happiness and contentment in the hands of others, especially his loved one who was addicted. Of course, as he later explained, the result was that he was perpetually disappointed and resentful.

I could relate to what he was saying. For a time in my life, my entire self-worth was dependent on how others behaved toward me. I could not be "okay" unless someone else approved of or accepted me. No matter what I did, I felt as though I wasn't good enough. I was touchy, easily offended, and miserable most of the time. It took a long time for me to make the connection that I was misplacing my personal power and reinforcing a sense of helplessness that was no longer real or necessary. In short, I was not taking responsibility for my own life or my own well-being. Instead of loving myself, I was prolonging my victimhood.

Through prayer, the Eucharist, and the Sacrament of Reconciliation, my self-awareness and understanding grew. I gradually came to realize that I was responsible for my own happiness and contentment! When I finally understood this truth, it was like a light went off in my soul—it felt like my own personal Independence Day! I was free from a bondage that I hadn't even known was enslaving me. I went from victim to victory in the Lord.

That victory was aided by my claiming, repeating, and meditating on Scripture passages that changed my thinking and my heart. Here are three that were most powerful for me:

A clean heart create for me, God;
   renew within me a steadfast spirit.
Do not drive me from before your face,
   nor take from me your holy spirit.
Restore to me the gladness of your salvation;
   uphold me with a willing spirit. (Psalm 51:12-14)

What will separate us from the love of Christ? Will anguish, or distress, or persecution, or famine, or nakedness, or peril, or the sword? . . . No, in all these things we conquer overwhelmingly through him who loved us. For I am convinced that neither death, nor life, nor angels, nor principalities, nor present things, nor future things, nor powers, nor height, nor depth, nor any other creature will be able to separate us from the love of God in Christ Jesus our Lord. (Romans 8:35, 37-39)

Whatever is true, whatever is honorable, whatever is just, whatever is pure, whatever is lovely, whatever is gracious, if there is any excellence and if there is anything worthy of praise, think about these things. Keep on doing what you have learned and received and heard and seen in me. Then the God of peace will be with you. (Philippians 4:8-9)

Opening the Door to Peace

One of my favorite quotes comes from the last line of a poem written by Amy Carmichael: "In acceptance lieth peace."[7] There is so much wisdom in that simple phrase, as well as hope. Accepting grace, accepting reality, and accepting responsibility will lead to peace in our lives. We want it for ourselves, and we want it for our loved one who is strug gling with addiction.

There are many ways to describe this state of peace and serenity that we long for. Here are a few: "a feeling of refreshing tranquility and an absence of tension or worry; the absence of mental stress or anxiety."[8] Notice that all of these descriptions are focused on the interior self. This condition of peace and serenity is not, in fact, contingent on what is going on around us or in the lives of other people. Peace is possible for us from the inside out, regardless of our circumstance. As Jesus said, "Peace I leave with you; my peace I give to you. Not as the world gives do I give it to you. Do not let your hearts be troubled or afraid" (John 14:27).

In twelve-step recovery programs, everything begins with acceptance: admitting and accepting our powerlessness over the addiction. Those of us who are praying for someone who is addicted must also accept that powerlessness. We can do nothing to control, change, or cure what is happening as a result of the addiction. Our mission is to accept and pray— and Jesus will do the rest.

Week One: Claiming the Grace

Reflection: Hebrews 4:16 (ESV)

> Let us then with confidence draw near to the throne of grace, that we may receive mercy and find grace to help in time of need.

Lectio Divina: How will you receive God's mercy this week? How will you share that mercy with others?

"Lord Jesus, I ask you to come into my life and my heart right now, just as they are. Even as I struggle with feelings of hurt, hopelessness, confusion, fear, anxiety, anger, or apathy, *I praise you* and claim the grace that you want to give me through this present situation. I claim the promise of a new freedom and a new happiness. I ask you to wrap me in your protection, fill me with your wisdom, and guide me with your hand of grace each and every day. Amen."

"Lord Jesus, wrap your loving arms around _____. I know that it will be by grace that _____ will be set free from addiction. I trust in your perfect timing to make it so. In a special way, I ask the Blessed Mother to watch over _____, for she is the perfect channel of your grace, and her motherly protection is a special gift that you have given to us all. Amen."

Week Two: Accepting Reality

Reflection: 2 Corinthians 12:7-9

A thorn in the flesh was given to me . . . to keep me from being too elated. Three times I begged the Lord about this, that it might leave me, but he said to me, *"My grace is sufficient for you, for power is made perfect in weakness."* (emphasis added)

Lectio Divina: How will you accept your weaknesses? How will you accept the weaknesses of the one who is addicted?

"Lord, I admit and accept that I am powerless over the addiction. Give me the grace to embrace the reality of my own limitations and to accept the truth of what is happening in my life and in the lives of those who are addicted. As I relinquish control, fill me with your Holy Spirit so that I may be a witness and an instrument of your peace. Amen."

"Lord, please help my loved one see the truth of his/her situation. Penetrate the layers of denial and defense and pierce his/her heart so that _____ is able to face the reality of the addiction and its dire consequences. Send the Holy Spirit to continually knock on _____'s heart so that the Spirit's clarity and truth can triumph! Amen."

Week Three: Taking Responsibility for Ourselves

Reflection: 1 Timothy 4:14, 15-16

> Do not neglect the gift you have. . . . Be diligent in these matters, be absorbed in them, so that your progress may be evident to everyone. Attend to yourself and to your teaching; persevere in both tasks, for by doing so you will save both yourself and those who listen to you.

Lectio Divina: How is the Lord leading you to "attend to yourself"?

"Sweet Jesus, please help me to keep the focus on you and me! Sometimes it is hard for me to love myself. Help me to sit quietly with you in prayer, and show me how to receive your love so that I might be better able to love myself and others. Lead me to grow in spiritual maturity. Heal me of any wounds that lead me to see myself as a victim or that drive me to resist your loving embrace. Keep me in your care all the days of my life. Amen."

"Lord, I trust in your providence and care of _____. I trust in your guidance in his/her life and vow to let the lessons of natural consequences unfold so that you can minister to and heal my loved one of addiction as you see fit. Amen."

Week Four: Opening the Door to Peace

Reflection: Philippians 4:7

> Then the peace of God that surpasses all understanding will guard your hearts and minds in Christ Jesus.

Lectio Divina: How will you receive God's peace this week?

"Lord, I want your peace! I need it to guard my heart and save my sanity. As I continue to take these steps toward freedom, fill me with the gift of your peace. I promise to open that gift each day with trust in your promise to provide and protect me and my loved ones always. Thank you, Jesus, for your promise of a peace that surpasses all understanding. Amen."

"Lord, I am willing to accept the situation that my loved one is in, just as it is at this present moment. Help me to understand that my acceptance does not condone or deny my loved one's addictive behavior but simply opens the door to peace and freedom for both of us. I trust deeply in your loving care for _____ and me, and I claim your grace for both of us. Amen."

Your Heart Prayer:

_____

_____

_____

_____

_____

_____

_____

_____

_____

_____

_____

_____

_____

_____

_____

_____

_____

_____

_____

Chapter Two

Hitting the Wall

You might feel as if you have hit the wall a thousand times when it comes to your loved one who is addicted. You may have "laid down the law," offered ultimatums, tried to set limits, washed your hands completely of the situation, or simply pretended that nothing was wrong. Yet deep in your heart, you know that something is very wrong and that you would probably do anything and everything in the world to make it right. Maybe you have already tried or are still trying to make things right.

I'm here to tell you that you will never succeed if what you are trying to do is stop the addiction. It's one of those things that *cannot be changed*, at least by you. There's a simple saying in Al-Anon that packs a powerful punch: "You didn't cause it, you can't control it, and you can't cure it." Until we come face-to-face with the full impact of what that means, we will never be free (and neither will our loved one).

You Didn't Cause It

There are as many reasons why someone becomes addicted as there are people who are addicted. Addiction is a very complex mind-body-spirit "dis-ease," as mentioned previously, and how it is manifested in the life of any given person is unique. The changes that take place in people as a result of addictions can be confusing and heartbreaking. Addiction can powerfully "take over" and distort a person's personality. It often erodes morality and leads people down degrading and deceitful roads that they would never travel if they were not addicts. As a result, addicts can become masters at manipulation and control. They often control others by holding them responsible for their own bad behavior. They shame, blame, and pull out all the stops to keep the focus off of them and onto others so that they don't have to take responsibility for the consequences of their addiction. There's a saying in recovery circles that people with addictions don't have relationships; instead, they take hostages. Maybe you can relate.

Once we know and accept this, we are free to no longer be held hostage by the misplaced guilt and anger that are heaped upon us. We don't have to accept responsibility, nor should we. We can no more cause someone to become addicted or to engage in addictive behaviors than we can create green cheese from moon rocks. Your actions or inactions cannot cause someone to become or remain or go deeper into any addiction. The Scriptures have something very instructive to say to us:

> Do not be deceived; God is not mocked, for you reap whatever you sow. If you sow to your own flesh, you will reap corruption from the flesh; but if you sow to the Spirit, you will reap eternal life from the Spirit. (Galatians 6:7-8, NRSV)

God is a good Father, and "reaping what we sow" is his way of helping us to learn from the natural consequences of our actions. When we step in front of God by trying to mitigate or erase the negative consequences brought about by the addiction as a way of trying to help or "support" the person, we are, in a sense, telling God that we know better than he does. We are derailing the lesson and prolonging the agony for everyone involved. As difficult as it is, we need to confess this and let the Spirit guide us, not our guilt or fear, when it comes to letting the consequences unfold naturally for our loved one.

You Can't Control It

Jane (not her real name) has been my acquaintance for many years, and we get together every couple of months to catch up. She has a lovely family with four grown sons and a husband who could win the prize for best husband of the year. She and her husband are retired and are financially able to travel anywhere they would like. But they don't. Most days it is difficult even to get Jane out of the house because she is consumed with worry and anxiety over her youngest son, who is on drugs and has been for almost seven years.

It truly has been a nightmarish ride for the whole family, but Jane, in particular, has been deeply enmeshed in the relationship, which can best be defined as "codependent." Melody Beattie, who wrote the breakthrough book entitled *Codependent No More: How to Stop Controlling Others and Start Caring for Yourself*, offers this definition of codependency: "A codependent person is one who has let another person's behavior affect him or her, and who is obsessed with controlling that person's behavior."[9]

Jane's whole personality has changed, and her appearance has become more and more disheveled. Her other children have distanced themselves or have been forced into distance because of Jane's complete preoccupation with her youngest son's behavior. In one conversation I had with Jane, as I was actively listening and attempting to lead her to some awareness of her lack of control, I noticed a distinct pattern as she talked. Each time I pointed out how her efforts to control had failed, she started her next sentence with "Yeah, but . . . "

It was an indication that she wasn't hearing what I was saying and that she was not ready to relinquish the idea that she could control anything about her son's situation. I counted twenty-seven "Yeah, buts" before our luncheon was over! Here are just a few of them.

"Yeah, but . . .

he needs me to help him."
he can't do this on his own."
how is he supposed to survive? He doesn't have any money."
it wasn't his fault this time."
I know if he just had a better job, things would be different."
the judge wouldn't listen to his side of the story."
the treatment center is only out for our money; they don't care."
I shouldn't have been so hard on him when he was a kid."
I'm the only one left who will listen to him or who understands him."
I'm his mother and I can't turn my back on him!"

"Yeah, buts" reveal that we are still trying to change things that cannot be changed. They indicate an internal set of beliefs and a stance that says, "I can and I must do something to make the situation better right now." They mean that we are still operating out of desperation with a solution that will never work. "Yeah, buts" keep us stuck trying to control instead of hitting that wall and admitting that we are completely unable to make people change what they cannot or do not want to change.

Before hitting that wall, we need to become aware of the many ways we try to control others: we do too much, we do too little, we give the silent treatment, we threaten, we complain, we get sick, we act helpless, we blame, we yell, we rage, we dominate, we withdraw, we ignore, we cajole and give lots of advice. We can also arrange, orchestrate, manipulate, and find solutions for other people's problems. We lie, cover up, and provide excuses, explanations, and rationalizations. We pretend nothing's wrong or we're convinced everything's wrong. We deny, push, become a victim, play God, go bankrupt, give in and give up, a hundred times a day. And this is just the short list!

We can engage in these behaviors subtly or outrageously, but whatever we do, we do it because we nurture the false belief that what we do or don't do can make someone else do what we want them to do or think they should do—which is to stop the addictive behavior that is causing so much pain.

But we can't.

You Can't Cure It

There has been an evolution in our understanding of addiction as an actual disease process that substantially alters and disrupts the normal chemistry and working of the brain. For example, we know through PET scans that brain changes occur when cocaine addicts merely watch videos of people using cocaine. Such scans have found similar changes in dopamine receptors in the brains of drug addicts, compulsive gamblers, and overeaters who are obese. In fact, "just about any deeply pleasurable activity—sex, eating, Internet use—has the potential to become addictive and destructive" for those who are susceptible to the disease of addiction.[10]

In essence, a substance such as a drug or an activity such as eating or shopping or gambling can act as a trigger and start the aberrant brain changes for someone with a predisposition to addiction. Additionally, those brain changes remain even after the substance or activity is removed or stopped. That is why the "cure" for addiction is a lifelong commitment to meeting the challenges posed by those physical changes. These challenges include but are not limited to intense cravings, chemical imbalances in the brain, and the potential for the addiction disease process to "pick up where it left off" even after years of abstinence.

Clearly, when we seek healing for our loved one with an addiction, we are seeking a healing of mind, body, and spirit. All the dimensions of a person are compromised by the disease of addiction. It is commonly stated that if the symptoms of the disease are left untreated and addiction is left to run its course, it will lead to jail, insanity, or death, or all three. Nothing we do or don't do personally can cure an addiction. But with our prayers and an infusion of faith, we can hope for a fourth option: recovery.

Do You Want to Be Well?

So what does recovery look like, anyway? What is your vision of restoration for the person you know who is addicted? Have you ever considered that your version might be very different from God's? Have you ever considered that your expectations might even be lower than the Lord's?

Sometimes we get comfortable with our chaos. As much as we may lament the way things are or wish that they were different for ourselves and the person with the addiction, we may not have a true or clear vision of anything else. We may not know what recovery is or what it would look like. I have often revisited the parable of the beggar at the pool of Bethesda:

> Now there is in Jerusalem at the Sheep [Gate] a pool called in Hebrew Bethesda, with five porticoes. In these lay a large number of ill, blind, lame, and crippled. One man was there who had been ill for thirty-eight years. When Jesus saw him lying there and knew that he had been ill for a long time, he said to him, "Do you want to be well?" The sick man answered him, "Sir, I have no one to put me into the pool when the water is stirred up; while I am on my way, someone else gets down there before me." Jesus said to him, "Rise, take up your mat, and walk." (John 5:2-8)

In this encounter, Jesus asks a very important question: "Do you want to be well?" Each and every one of us, at some point in our lives, will have to answer that question for ourselves before Jesus. As sinners in need of redemption, we all need to be made well in some way or another, and we can't answer the question for anyone but ourselves. It is a moment of grace when we discover that Jesus is asking us this question, and our reply is our first step toward recovery and restoration.

It seems so natural that the beggar would say yes right away, given the fact that he had been lying there for thirty-eight years, but he doesn't. Instead, he offers reasons why it hasn't happened yet. Some might call it an excuse, but what he is saying reveals that he still believes that he can do it on his own power. That's why he gives Jesus reasons why he hasn't been able to heal himself or why someone else hasn't done it for him!

Fortunately, for him and for us, Jesus overlooks these protestations and perseveres in his intention to heal the beggar, even on the Sabbath. Jesus came to restore us to sanity and set the captives free, even for those of us who aren't too sure what that means!

While the beggar is focused on a cure that will take place outside of himself, Jesus has another type of healing in mind. The beggar would have been satisfied with a dip in the healing waters and calling it a day, while Jesus is offering a total transformation of mind, body, and soul—a complete restoration. He desires to make this beggar completely whole, just as he desires to restore you and your loved one to wholeness and freedom from addiction.

The healing that we wish for, pray for, bargain for, cry out for from the depths of our hearts may not be as complete as the one that Jesus has in mind. It is a cure that only he can administer as the almighty Physician and Healer, and it will not be just for your loved one but for you as well. The beautiful part about hitting a wall and surrendering our control is the movement in our souls that takes place as *we come to believe* that restoration and sanity are possible for us and our loved one. It is the budding of hope in our hearts. Even if we are like the beggar and are too scared, scarred, jaded, or exhausted to claim that healing right away, we are coming to believe, and that is enough.

It is enough to know that we are on a journey and that we are not alone. It is enough to know that we don't have the solution and that we don't even have to know what the solution might be. There is a power that is greater than ourselves, and we can trust ourselves and our loved one to the Lord.

Week One: I Didn't Cause It

Reflection: Isaiah 41:10

> Do not fear: I am with you;
>   do not be anxious: I am your God.
> I will strengthen you, I will help you,
>   I will uphold you with my victorious right hand.

Lectio Divina: How will you let the Lord strengthen you this week?

"Lord Jesus, help me to trust in God the Father and his goodness to teach and care for my loved one who is addicted. Give me peace as I let go of trying to lessen the consequences of his/her actions or addictions. Release me from feelings of guilt, shame, fear, or compulsion, and replace them with a firm resolve to stay focused on you and the presence of the Holy Spirit within me. Holy Spirit, come! Amen."

"Heavenly Father, I entrust my loved one to your care. Please penetrate the denial and effects of addiction and reach down with your grace, comfort, and saving love. I know that you love _____ more than I ever could, and you understand this situation more than I ever will. Give _____ the grace to receive your remedy and to respond to your love. Amen."

Week Two: I Can't Control It

Reflection: Psalm 34:19-20

> The LORD is close to the brokenhearted,
>   saves those whose spirit is crushed.
> Many are the troubles of the righteous,
>   but the LORD delivers him from them all.

Lectio Divina: How will I stay close to the Lord this week?

"Lord, show me how to take good and gentle care of myself. Sometimes I feel so lost, insecure, and out of touch with who I am. Heal me from any codependent tendencies, and help me to root out behaviors that are self-defeating, draining, and damaging to my life. Help me to make a daily decision of self-care and respect, in your name. Amen."

"Jesus, I release all control of _____'s addiction to you. I relinquish my role in his/her recovery and acknowledge your power to restore his/her life to sanity. Amen."

Week Three: I Can't Cure It

Reflection: Romans 8:11

> If the Spirit of the one who raised Jesus from the dead dwells in you, the one who raised Christ from the dead will give life to your mortal bodies also, through his Spirit that dwells in you.

Lectio Divina: What areas of your life need tending by the Great Physician?

"Lord, you are our almighty Physician and Healer, and I believe in your desire to bind up and restore us. I praise you for your power to bring about complete and total healing, peace, and sanity to my life and the lives of those I love who are struggling. Amen."

"Lord, you alone know the depth of pain and the wounds that drive _____'s addiction, and you alone can bring complete healing. Jesus, I release _____ into your capable hands to be healed. Amen."

Week Four: Yes, I Want to Be Made Well

Reflection: Proverbs 3:7-8

Do not be wise in your own eyes,
    fear the LORD and turn away from evil;
This will mean health for your flesh
    and vigor for your bones.

Lectio Divina: What weariness will you bring to the heart of Jesus to be restored?

"Lord, if there are areas in my own life that need to be healed, please reveal them to me so that I may respond, *'Yes, Lord, I want to be made well.'* Please heal me too! Amen."

"Dear Lord, I know that your love is stronger than any addiction and that it is the desire of your heart to bring freedom and healing to _____. Please help him/her to let go of any excuses or barriers that are getting in the way of the flow of your grace. Give _____ the courage to say yes to a complete healing from addiction. Amen."

Your Heart Prayer:

_____

_____

_____

_____

_____

_____

_____

_____

_____

_____

_____

_____

_____

_____

_____

_____

_____

_____

_____

_____

CHAPTER THREE

The Courage to Change

The desktop wallpaper on my computer features a smiley face with a dialogue bubble that says, "I can!" In big, bold letters, the caption reads, *"Feed your faith and your fears will starve to death!"* In many ways this is the definition of courage. It is not the absence of fear but the willingness to keep moving forward in faith even when you are feeling afraid.

Sometimes courage requires a few interim steps, however. In fact, the third line of the serenity prayer is a very powerful one, and the most important word in it is not "courage" but "should." The popularized version of this prayer leaves out "should" and states, "[Grant me the] courage to change the things I can." However, the original prayer states, "[Grant me the] courage to change the things that *should* be changed" (emphasis added).

This tiny difference is a key aspect of our freedom, and it is worth exploring further.

Choices and Change

Resisting what *should* be changed is often at the root of our unhappiness. I'll say it again because it is important: resisting what *should* be changed is often at the root of our unhappiness. It is a supreme temptation (and I believe a tool of the evil one) to hyper-focus on what is impossible to change as a way for us to avoid the fear or responsibility of changing what is realistically within our control. It keeps us floundering and confused about what can and truly needs to be changed. Some people spend years, even an entire lifetime, stuck right there.

I remember one of the first Al-Anon meetings I attended. I was embarrassed and ashamed because I was so desperate and worn out from trying to find a way to stop my mother from drinking (and raging). Every attempt had fallen short, and I was terrified as I walked into the room, convinced that everyone there would judge and condemn me and think I was a complete failure.

It didn't take me long to realize that my thinking and perspective were distorted. People were telling me that it wasn't my job to change my mother's behavior and that it was no wonder I was exhausted. They patiently and repeatedly helped me to understand that my energy needed to go into what could and should be changed *by me* in order to make my life better. What needed to be changed the most was *within* me. It took me awhile to release my grip on the need to focus on my mother, but after I got through the initial indignation, denial, and resentment over what they were saying, I started to feel relieved and excited about making some positive changes *just for me*.

What can and should be changed? Any behavior or pattern of thinking or acting to which we cling that is self-defeating, that keeps us stuck or resentful, that perpetuates our lack of healthy boundaries, or that allows others to violate or victimize us. Notice there is nothing about our loved one with the addiction here. It is only possible for us to change what is within us or in the environment that surrounds us.

Ever since Eve ate the forbidden fruit, we've been wrestling with the consequences of what it means to try to be "like God" (cf. Genesis 3:5). God is the one who knows all things, but sometimes we think we do. We think we know what is best for others; we think we have far more control than we really do. In essence, we don't know our place, and we abuse our power, which is, again, a result of the fall. These tendencies are what keep us perpetually trying to change what cannot be changed instead of changing what should be changed.

Just as Eve discovered, we must also learn that life is all about choices. We are free to make good ones or bad ones, but *we all have choices*. At one point in their life, your loved one made a bad choice. And then they made another one and another one, until their freedom was compromised by the addiction process. Now, to change that downhill slide, your loved one will have to make another series of choices. You can't make those choices for that person, and you can't change the consequences of the ones they have already made. Not only can't you, but you shouldn't even try.

So many times we relinquish our responsibility to make choices or are unaware of our freedom to make good choices for ourselves. One of the major things that keeps us stuck or prompts us to keep making bad choices is shame. Guilt and shame are often linked to one another, but they are quite different. We feel guilty about what we have done, but shame is about rejecting who we are. It penetrates to the core of our being. Intense feelings of inadequacy, inferiority, or self-hatred fueled by shame cause us to want to hide and cover up (like Adam and Eve) or hold us back from making the decisions we need to make.

Making a Decision

The first decision we need to be willing to make is the one that will lead us out of shame. Step Three of the twelve-step recovery programs says this: "Made a decision to turn our will and our lives over to the care of God as we understood Him."

The nature of patterns, especially patterns that reinforce shame, is that they are largely unconscious. We engage in behaviors over and over again because what drives us or motivates us to act hasn't been brought into our awareness yet, or we simply haven't learned any other way of behaving. We all do the best we can at any given moment in time. Yet when we make a decision, it is by its very definition a conscious act. In fact, Merriam-Webster defines a decision as "a choice that you make about something after thinking about it."

When we make a decision to try and change someone else or try to stop them from behaving in a certain way, we are making a decision that will keep us in bondage to futility and failure. But when we make a decision to turn our will and our lives over to God, we are making a decision that will lead us to authentic freedom and victory. Which will you choose?

It's not that easy, you say? You're right—it's not. Getting free can be infinitely more difficult than staying stuck. "Being controlled by others [and their addictions] is a safe prison," write Christian psychologists Henry Cloud and John Townsend. "We know where all the rooms are!"[11] And, I might add, we also know the rules. But Jesus is in the business of setting us free from our worries, our guilt, and our past pain and patterns.

Sometimes when I look at the cross and reflect on the open arms of Jesus, I am reminded that he is always waiting for us to run into his embrace, to trust him in the midst of every storm and sadness. He never gets tired of waiting, not for us and not for our loved ones who are addicted. God cares—isn't that a beautiful thought? Have you ever stopped to think about what God's tender care is really like? Have you ever considered that God cares about you no matter how scared you may be, no matter how tired or hopeless or resentful, no matter what little faith you may have left? He cares deeply, with a heart full of mercy and compassion. His care is perfect and infinite, and it includes every person in the world.

It can be difficult to receive care from others, especially God. We may wonder deep down if we can truly trust the Lord. We may not know how to let him or anyone else in our lives care for us. We may be uncertain about how to take gentle care of ourselves. Maybe we have experienced so many relationships in which we felt or were truly uncared for that we've concluded that it's hopeless to even try to let someone care for us. This is the evil one at his best. He wants you to give up and stay stuck in the futility of trying to take care of everything and everyone on your own, without regard for your own legitimate needs.

A truism from Al-Anon states, "Nothing changes if nothing changes." For us, learning how to let God care for us and releasing our will and our lives over to him are changes that will require not just courage but determination, prayer, and grace. One prayer that calls upon the care of the Lord is the Our Father, and it's something we pray all the time without thinking about it.

But when we pray, "Thy kingdom come, thy will be done on earth as it is in heaven," what we are really asking is for God to take the reins of our lives and to be the one in control. We make the decision to let him be in control because we know we can't do it for ourselves. Our control is like a big, bold red "X" that stamps out any hope of peace or serenity in our lives.

However, when we turn our lives over to God, things happen—good things. We can trust him to bring those good things about in his perfect way and in the timing that is just right for us and our loved ones. We don't know the day-to-day details of his *grand* plan, but we can trust that it is good because we are told this in Scripture:

> For surely I know the plans I have for [insert your name/your loved one's name], says the LORD, plans for your welfare and not for harm, to give you a future with hope. Then when you call upon me and come and pray to me, I will hear you. When you search for me, you will find me; if you seek me with all your heart, I will let you find me, says the LORD. (Jeremiah 29:11-14, NRSV)

This holds true for you and for anyone who is addicted. When you release control of all of your plans and all your desired outcomes for your loved one, you make room for God's solution to take hold. And his solution is infinitely better than anything you or I could even imagine.

Where Courage Comes In

As Catholics, we are blessed beyond measure to have the sacraments to aid us. They are the permanent and tangible way we experience the fullness of God's love, mercy, and hope here on earth. We encounter Jesus immediately and completely through the sacraments so that from him, we will gain all the courage we need on our journey to serenity and peace.

I think of courage as a staircase. We take one step at a time, and every time we renew our baptismal vows, as well as every time we receive the Eucharist, go to Confession, or receive the Anointing of the Sick, we are given the strength and determination to climb the next step. I believe it is the Holy Spirit who surrounds us on this climb. He goes before us, gently beckoning us and calling us forward out of our shame and sorrow with that still, small voice within us. He stands behind us, ready to catch us when we fall or when we simply need a little push to keep striving for peace and serenity. He walks next to us, encouraging and assuring us that we are never alone.

In prayer, the Holy Spirit is always present on this road to courage, and we can call upon him on behalf of our loved ones. We can offer Masses for them, we can dedicate a holy hour to them, and we can stand in proxy at a healing Mass. Above all, we can meet our merciful and forgiving Lord in the Sacrament of Reconciliation, where he will minister to our brokenness and fill us with the courage to go on.

One final thought on courage: it takes just as much courage to quit an addiction as it does to let God take the lead in our lives. You can't climb that staircase of courage for your loved one, and your loved one can't climb it for you. In fact, these are two entirely different sets of stairs! Remember, courage is taking your own staircase.

Week One: Choices

Reflection: Romans 10:11

For the scripture says, "No one who believes in him will be put to shame."

Lectio Divina: What is the role of shame in your life? How will you release it?

"Lord, I need your wisdom, guidance, and grace to follow through on the choices I must make that will lead to serenity and peace. Strengthen me through your sacraments so that I might feed my faith and starve my fears. Amen."

"My Lord, help my loved one to make good choices and to come to a personal acceptance of your love. Deliver my loved one from all evil and purify all of his/her desires. Amen."

Week Two: Changes

Reflection: Psalm 139:23-24 (NIV)

Search me, God and know my heart;
    test me and know my anxious thoughts.
See if there is any offensive way in me,
    and lead me in the way everlasting.

Lectio Divina: What do you want Jesus to know about your heart? What do you want to say to him?

"Oh my Jesus, sometimes I take on more than I should. Sometimes I resist change that could bring me to a greater good. Still, in every situation, I know that you love me and want what is best. Whatever I'm lacking, Lord, I trust in you to provide the rest. Amen."

"Lord, unlock _____ from the burden of shame so that he/she no longer needs to hide from you. Quell the anxieties and fears that seem to surround my loved one, and penetrate the negativity that fuels the addiction. Amen."

Week Three: Decisions

Reflection: Acts 4:12

"There is no salvation through anyone else, nor is there any other name under heaven given to the human race by which we are to be saved."

Lectio Divina: What does the name of Jesus mean to you?

"Dear Lord, I vow to turn my will and my life over to you. I know that you are the Savior of the world and the Lord of my life. Fill me with your wisdom, and help me to receive your loving kindness and care. Amen."

"Lord, lead my loved one to safety one day at a time in your Spirit. I am grateful that _____ is in your care and that you will cover my loved one in your mercy and keep watch over his/her soul. Amen."

Week Four: Courage

Reflection: Romans 12:2

Do not conform yourselves to this age but be transformed by the renewal of your mind, that you may discern what is the will of God, what is good and pleasing and perfect.

Lectio Divina: How does your mind need to be transformed?

"Lord, send your Holy Spirit to bring me clarity and an undivided heart. Give me the courage to change what I should, and help me discern the path I should go and the actions I should take. If I am undecided, give me the grace to simply wait and rest in you. Amen."

"Holy Lord, your love sustains us and surrounds us. Fill my loved one with the courage to change what he/she should and to embrace the good life that you died to give us. Amen."

Your Heart Prayer:

_____

_____

_____

_____

_____

_____

_____

_____

_____

_____

_____

_____

_____

_____

_____

_____

_____

_____

_____

_____

Chapter Four

Searching for Clarity

When I was seven, I went on a boat ride with my father and some friends on an unfamiliar lake. We motored to a remote section to do some fishing, and when we started to head back, the motor quit. At the same time, black clouds started rolling in as a storm kicked up. As we struggled with the oars in the swirling waves, I started to cry.

My father, in an effort to calm me, told me to focus my eyes on a tiny speck on the distant horizon. He explained that the more I fixed my eyes on the speck, the bigger it would get— almost like magic. He was right! As I turned my attention to it, the "speck" slowly came into clearer view and I recognized it as our cozy camp. Safe at last, I can still remember the sense of relief I felt as I stepped out of that boat.

Wisdom is like that speck in the distance. When we turn our attention to it, when we focus on God's wisdom, not on our own or on all that is tumultuous or stormy in our lives, he gives us clearer vision and leads us to safety and to higher ground. Wisdom brings clarity to our hearts and our minds, and when we pray for God's wisdom, he always delivers on those prayers.

One way wisdom comes to us is as one of the gifts of the Holy Spirit. Wisdom as a gift of the Holy Spirit is not like human wisdom, which we gain through experience and trial and error. Nor is it an accumulation of knowledge or understanding. Instead, it is a supernatural gift from God that enables us to see things as he does. This is how Pope Francis describes this gift:

Wisdom is precisely this: it is the grace of being able *to see everything with the eyes of God.* It is simply this: it is to see the world, to see situations, circumstances, problems, everything through God's eyes. This is wisdom. Sometimes we see things according to our liking or according to the condition of our heart, with love or with hate, with envy . . . No, this is not God's perspective. Wisdom is what the Holy Spirit works in us so as to enable us to see things with the eyes of God. This is the gift of wisdom.[12]

I wonder how the view of our horizons might change if we were looking through the eyes of God?

An Important Reminder

Practically speaking, when it comes to addiction, knowing what can and cannot be changed—and having the wisdom to know the difference—is a matter of seeing things correctly and erecting healthy boundaries. Wisdom leads us to a firm understanding of what our limitations are when it comes to if, when, and how to help in the face of any addiction. Wisdom also helps us to be clear with the person who is addicted concerning how we want to be treated. Healthy boundaries keep us safe when the storms start to rage.

Addiction can lead good people to do some pretty bad things. We don't have to accept or condone those things or allow them to wound us to the core. We don't ever have to, nor should we ever, tolerate any forms of physical or emotional abuse or violence. We are never helping the person with an addiction when we allow ourselves to be abused physically, verbally, emotionally, or financially. It's an unwise and unhealthy boundary violation that simply keeps the storm raging.

Sometimes we may need to keep our distance, to detach, disengage, and remove ourselves from an active relationship with someone who is addicted. This can be a heroic act of compassion when safety is the concern. It is a spiritual work of mercy, that of "ransoming the captive." By stepping out of the situation, you are setting yourself free.

Another Step toward Freedom

The Church has always taught us about the need to focus on our own behavior so that we can get free of the habits and sins that can obscure our sight. In recovery circles, this is called a personal moral inventory; for Catholics, it is known as an examination of conscience. An examination of conscience can be made at any time; many people examine their conscience and ask God for forgiveness at the end of each day.

Catholics often prepare for the Sacrament of Confession using an examination of conscience. There are short and longer versions of this examination, which is usually made up of a list of questions that we ask ourselves. When we go to meet the merciful Jesus in the Sacrament of Reconciliation through the priest, we tell him with a contrite heart our sins, mistakes, shortcomings, and burdens. In return, we receive grace, mercy, absolution, and freedom. Indeed, we are healed from the inside out! It's a beautiful encounter that fills us with hope and gives us the strength, courage, and clarity to press on in our lives and our prayers.

In the Gospel of Luke, Jesus instructs us to "be merciful, just as your Father is merciful" (6:36), but it's often hard to muster up mercy in the face of addiction. For many people, the emotional response to another's addiction is hurt and anger. Lots of times, resentment isn't too far behind. Mercy can be defined as "a moral virtue that prompts one to have compassion for and to be moved toward alleviating the suffering of those who are in spiritual or temporal need."[13] The *Catechism* defines "works of mercy" as "charitable actions by which we come to the aid of our neighbors in their bodily and spiritual needs" (Glossary). Certainly, there is no one in greater need of the corporal or spiritual works of mercy than someone who is in bondage to addiction.

Nevertheless, mercy, as a virtue, is not something that comes naturally to us. We need to pray for it, cultivate it, and sow its seeds in our lives in order for it to bear fruit in our relationships. Confession is our tool for doing that because it prepares the soil of our own hearts to take up our prayerful mission of mercy on behalf of the addict. When we humble our hearts in the Sacrament of Reconciliation, we are healed through God's mercy. In turn, we are then called to be merciful toward others in the hopes that they, too, might be healed.

The beautiful image of the lighthouse on the cover of this book is a perfect reminder of what Proverbs 18:10 says: "The name of the LORD is a strong tower; / the just run to it and are safe."

When we pray our loved ones through the storm of addiction, God's word assures us that as we call on the name of Jesus for wisdom and clarity, he will send down his Holy Spirit in a special way for the brokenhearted and hurting. Most people who are caught up in addictions are drowning in fear and shame. Our prayers are their lifelines to the strong tower of Jesus and his healing love.

Week One: Wisdom

Reflection: James 1:5-6

> But if any of you lacks wisdom, he should ask God who gives to all generously and ungrudgingly, and he will be given it. But he should ask in faith, not doubting, for the one who doubts is like a wave of the sea that is driven and tossed about by the wind.

Lectio Divina: What doubts do you have? How will you hand them over to Jesus?

"Heavenly Father, you give us all such wonderful gifts, and I am grateful! Strengthen my faith, remove my doubts, and fill me with your wisdom so that I might see my loved ones, especially those with addictions, with the eyes of your heart. Amen."

"Dear Father God, look after _____ in this time of addiction. Send your angels of mercy to protect and instruct him/her in your ways. In a special way, send Mary, our mother and teacher of grace, to penetrate the fog of addiction with her intercessory prayers and lead my loved one to the clarity of recovery. Amen."

Week Two: Focus

Reflection: Hebrews 12:1-2

> Let us rid ourselves of every burden and sin that clings to us and persevere in running the race that lies before us while keeping our eyes fixed on Jesus, the leader and perfecter of faith.

Lectio Divina: What are the ways you can keep your eyes fixed on Jesus this week?

"Dear Lord, when I feel that I am drowning and being dragged under by the storms of life, help me to keep my eyes, mind, and heart fixed on you. Give me the strength to erect healthy boundaries so that when you call me to the back of the boat to join you in your peace, I will! When you ask me to rest my head upon your heart, I will! When you invite me to lay down my burdens and trust you, I will! Amen."

"Lord, I know that you are calling out to my loved one, that *you* are the safety and shelter that _____ seeks. Please be like a lighthouse in his/her storm of addiction. May _____ look up in a moment of grace and see only you as the way, the truth, and the restorer of life. Amen."

Week Three: Looking Within

Reflection: 1 John 1:9

If we acknowledge our sins, he is faithful and just and will forgive our sins and cleanse us from every wrongdoing.

Lectio Divina: How do you need to be cleansed?

"Dear Jesus, thank you for your gifts of forgiveness and mercy. Prepare me to meet you in the Sacrament of Confession, and give me the courage to lay down my burdens at your feet and leave them there. Dear Lord, set me free. Amen."

"Oh Lord, you are the path to freedom. Addiction keeps us locked up in a prison of self, and your mercy is the only key! Surround _____ with your love, and instill in him/her a desire to be cleansed by your saving grace. Penetrate the hardness of my loved one's heart, infiltrate the chaos of his/her mind, and enlighten the darkness in his/her soul. Restore _____ to a state of grace. Amen."

Week Four: A Mission of Mercy

Reflection: 2 Timothy 1:9

> He saved us and called us to a holy life, not according to our works but according to his own design and the grace bestowed on us in Christ Jesus before time began.

Lectio Divina: How has the Lord saved you?

"Sweet Jesus, my Savior, have mercy on me, a sinner, and by your grace help me to be merciful to others, especially to those who reject me or cause me pain. Your mercy, O Lord, brings hope to the hopeless and life to the dying. Let me be an instrument of your mercy in the world and in my life. Amen."

"My God and my All, from your wounded heart, you pour out your mercy upon us. Restore in _____ a desire for a holy life and lead him/her back to you. Amen."

Your Heart Prayer:

_____

_____

_____

_____

_____

_____

_____

_____

_____

_____

_____

_____

_____

_____

_____

_____

_____

_____

_____

_____

_____

CHAPTER FIVE

One Day at a Time

L iving in the present moment is an absolute necessity if we are to enjoy our lives and the gifts that God wants to give us each day. For many of us, this is a very difficult task, whether we are touched by addiction or not. Without even realizing it, we may be clinging to the past and the way things used to be or be influenced by it in a way that keeps us from growing. There is also the temptation to live in the future. Instead of living one day at a time, we are always one step ahead, either fearful or driven, trying to anticipate or control events that may never come to pass. But what would life be like if we committed to living just for today?

When we release our grip on the past and the future, we are able to stand before God each day with open arms, mind, and heart to receive every blessing and grace we need.

Do you remember what it was like to be a child and have no concept of time? Do you remember playing outside when a day stretched on forever and you soaked in every second of sunlight, hoping that it would never end? What freedom and joy!

How is it that as we grow up, the days become shorter and seem to slip through our fingers? Why is it that as we lay down our heads each night, we can hardly recall where we have been or what we've been doing but only know that we are exhausted and depleted? It doesn't have to be this way. We can be restored to that childlike state; in fact, it is what God desires of us and for us. He said, "Truly I tell you, unless you change and become like children, you will never enter the kingdom of heaven" (Matthew 18:3, NRSV).

That should make it abundantly clear that we are meant to live one day at a time! Yet how do we slow down our minds and lives enough to do that? Thankfully, our faith offers a rich treasury of ways, and there are many traditions and saints that can help us.

Our Daily Offering

One of the best ways to live one day at a time is to begin by dedicating our day to the Lord. Many Catholics start the day with a short prayer known as a daily offering. Here is a traditional one:

> O Jesus, through the Immaculate Heart of Mary, I offer you my prayers, works, joys, and sufferings of this day for all the intentions of your Sacred Heart, in union with the Holy Sacrifice of the Mass throughout the world, for the salvation of souls, the reparation of sins, the reunion of all Christians, and in particular for the intentions of the Holy Father this month. Amen.[14]

This is a beautiful prayer because it connects us with our whole human family and the communion of saints, both living and dead. It also unites us all in the Sacred Heart of Jesus. This prayer brings into focus a purpose for our day: to live it for the sake of others out of love for Jesus, with a desire to quench the thirst of his heart for every soul. It doesn't get any better than that!

There are also many daily prayers for and from people in twelve-step recovery programs. Here's one example, entitled "For Another Day":

Thank You, dear God, for another day,
The chance to live in a decent way,
To feel again the joy of living,
And happiness that comes from giving.
Thank You for friends who can understand
And the peace that flows from Your loving hand.
Help me to wake to the morning sun
With the prayer, "Today, Thy will be done"
For with Your help I will find the way.
Thank You again, dear God, for another day.[15]

You can be certain that any sincere daily offering that you give to Jesus will be multiplied by him tenfold! I think the key is to keep it simple and centered on gratitude, because the daily offering prayer is really a reminder that your life is a gift from God, and how you live it is your gift back to him.

The Little Way

St. Thérèse of Lisieux is known as the saint of the little way and spiritual childhood. She is also a Doctor of the Church and a master trainer in how to live one day at a time. She placed all of her trust in Jesus as a little child does in its mother. In a letter to her sister Celine, she wrote, "It is not, then, intelligence and talents that Jesus has come to seek here below. . . . He cherishes simplicity."[16] She truly embraced the promise of

Jesus when he said, "Blessed are the poor in spirit, / for theirs is the kingdom of heaven" (Matthew 5:3).

God's kingdom comes to earth and its peace and joy reign in our lives when we endeavor to live one day at a time with a childlike spirit of trust in Jesus. As we grow into adulthood, we become experts in how to worry. Life teaches us this lesson, but the Holy Spirit can help us to *unlearn* it. Our worry and anxiety flow mostly from a faulty belief that we should have done things differently or that we need to do something more in order to be happy, secure, or safe in life. Worry is a direct result of not living in the moment. It also comes from believing that we, our own power, are solely responsible for everything that happens. Reality couldn't be further from the truth! As St. Thérèse explains,

> From the moment I understood that it was impossible for me to do anything by myself, the task imposed upon me no longer appeared difficult. I felt that the only thing necessary was to unite myself more and more to Jesus and that *"all things will be given to you besides."*[17]

Addiction makes our lives so complicated. The spirituality of St. Thérèse is like a lifeline in the storm. If we focus on the present, we won't miss the wisdom, comfort, and peace that the Lord wants to give us. We will feel his presence by our side, and our "What-if's?" will turn into "What now, Lord?" We can learn a childlike confidence that expects nothing but the best from our good and gracious God.

Moment to Moment

Recovery is a *lifelong* commitment and process, and I remember in the early days of mine when the idea of living one day at a time seemed not only terrifying but impossible. That's when I decided to take it one hour at a time. I distinctly remember sitting in a college classroom and looking at the clock while thanking God under my breath for helping me get through the previous hour without completely falling apart! And then there were days when even an hour was too much. That gave way to living life as a moment-by-moment "cliff-hanger," clinging to Jesus' garments much like the woman with the issue of blood.

As I've grown in recovery and spirit, that moment-to-moment approach to life has become an interior spirituality that is now one of the best fruits of my recovery thus far. Today I live life, not anticipating or fearing doom and gloom and demise, but with an intentional expectation of receiving God's goodness *in every present moment*. It turns out that this is not a new discovery and that many saints have employed this approach to life.

Fr. Jean-Pierre de Caussade, a French Jesuit and spiritual director from the seventeenth century of whom little is known, has presented us with a spiritual classic that serves as a guidebook and resource for living this way. In *Abandonment to Divine Providence*, he encourages us to live in the "sacrament" of the present moment because "God speaks to every individual through what happens to them moment by moment."[18] He writes, "At every moment, God's will produces what is needful for the task in hand, and the simple soul, instructed by faith, finds everything as it should be. . . . It relies no longer on its own ideas to help it to bear the weariness and difficulties of the journey."[19]

If we sincerely take the Lord at his word and truly believe what he says, then abandoning ourselves to his perfect will in every moment of our lives makes perfect sense, even when our lives seem to be spiraling out of control. In fact, it is the *only* thing that makes sense! That's because "we know that all things work for good for those who love God, who are called according to his purpose" (Romans 8:28).

While at times we or our loved ones may live our lives outside of God's will, we are never beyond his love. "For those who abandon themselves to it," writes de Caussade, "God's love contains every good thing, and if you long for it with all your heart and soul it will be yours."[20] Keeping your focus on God's loving will in every moment is a sweet surrender and a way of life that brings great peace.

A Perfect Prayer

When the disciples asked Jesus how to pray, he gave them a perfect prayer. In the Our Father, there is tremendous wisdom for living one day at a time:

> Our Father, who art in heaven,
> Hallowed be thy name;
> Thy kingdom come, thy will be done
> On earth as it is in heaven.
> Give us this day our daily bread,
> And forgive us our trespasses.
> As we forgive those who trespass against us;

And lead us not into temptation,
But deliver us from evil. Amen.

As each day comes to an end, consider thoughtfully reflecting on each line of this prayer as a way of conducting an interior examination before retiring. Here's what I mean:

Our Father, who art in heaven, hallowed be thy name.
Calling out to God, remembering with reverence and respect that he alone is sovereign, puts our lives in perspective. We serve a God, and we are not him! He deserves our praise, no matter what is going on in our lives.

Thy kingdom come, thy will be done.
How well did we relinquish our control over people, circumstances, and situations today? How much did we trust and seek his will and not our own? Did we live moment to moment?

On earth as it is in heaven.
Were we mindful of the passing nature of our lives, and did we embrace a heavenly perspective instead of getting bogged down in worry, regret, or anxiety? Did we take anything for granted or settle for less in our conduct or behavior?

Give us this day our daily bread.
Did we live with a grateful heart today? Did we embrace the simple pleasures? Did we thank God for every good gift, everything that happened, and even thank him for our unmet needs and trials, knowing that he can and will work all things for our good?

And forgive us our trespasses.
Did we trust in God's mercy today? Did we seek prompt forgiveness when we did something wrong? Did we conduct ourselves with humility and gentleness and possess a contrite heart?

As we forgive those who trespass against us.
Were we quick to forgive today, giving others the benefit of the doubt? Can we let go of resentments, seek reconciliation, and offer mercy to those who have offended or hurt us? Will we let go of criticism, comparisons, and condemnation in our hearts?

And lead us not into temptation.
Did we avoid situations that could lead us into sin or cause others to sin? Are we mindful of our greatest temptations, and did we seek Jesus first?

But deliver us from evil.
Like St. Thérèse, did we make love our vocation today? Did we seek to be childlike, guileless, and holy? Did we stay grounded in God's love today?

Amen.
"Let it be so." Surrender this day to Jesus, give it to him as your gift, and go to sleep with confidence in his love and mercy for another day.

Living one day at a time assures us that we will offer an example and witness to those around us. People will look at us and think, "I want what she has!" Let us pray that they will be drawn to the calm and steady anchor that we know is Jesus living in our hearts moment to moment by his grace, and that they, too, will seek a new way of life.

Week One: Our Daily Offering

Reflection: Psalm 92:2-3

> It is good to give thanks to the LORD,
>> to sing praise to your name, Most High,
> To proclaim your love at daybreak,
>> your faithfulness in the night.

Lectio Divina: What is your humble offering to Jesus today?

"Lord, I join the communion of saints on heaven and earth to make the most of every day and to offer each one as a gift to you. I vow not to waste time in worry and distress, but to offer little sacrifices and to persevere in doing good deeds for the good of others and for your glory. Amen."

"Lord, please grant _____ another day, because with each new day, there is hope for recovery, conversion, and a new life in you. Renew me in my prayerful efforts, and touch _____'s heart. Make it childlike in trust and hope for a better way of living in the freedom you so long to give. Amen."

Week Two: The Little Way

Reflection: Psalm 131:1-2

> LORD, my heart is not proud;
>   nor are my eyes haughty.
> I do not busy myself with great matters,
>   with things too sublime for me.
> Rather, I have stilled my soul,
> Like a weaned child to its mother,
>   weaned is my soul.

Lectio Divina: What "great matters" are making you too busy?

"Holy Spirit, help me to learn a little way of living that draws me into the loving arms of my God. Help me to walk gently through each day with an awareness of Jesus by my side, who is there to help me and love me and keep me and my loved ones safe. Amen."

"Holy Spirit, help _____ to learn a new way of life that inspires a childlike confidence and dependence on you instead of any harmful substance or activity. I pray especially for the intercession of St. Thérèse for _____ to surrender to the loving arms of God for help, healing, and a one-day-at-a-time life of peace and joy. Amen."

Week Three: Moment to Moment

Reflection: Matthew 6:25, 27, 34

> [Jesus said,] "Do not worry about your life. . . . Can any of you by worrying add a single moment to your life-span? . . . Do not worry about tomorrow; tomorrow will take care of itself."

Lectio Divina: What worries have taken up residence in your heart?

"Lord, give me the grace to live my life surrendered to the sacrament of each present moment. Give me the desire to abandon myself to your will in every circumstance, knowing that your ways are perfect and loving, merciful and just. Jesus, I trust in you! Amen."

"Dear Lord, I pray for _____, who will never be outside of your love but who seems so lost right now. I pray that you will hold _____ in the palm of your hand each moment of his/her life. I surrender this addiction and circumstance to your holy will so that you can bring good from it. Jesus, I love your will! Amen."

Week Four: A Perfect Prayer

Reflection: Matthew 6:5, 6, 8

[Jesus said,] "When you pray, do not be like the hypocrites, who love to stand and pray in the synagogues and on street corners so that others may see them. . . . When you pray, go to your inner room, close the door, and pray to your Father in secret. . . . Your Father knows what you need before you ask him."

Lectio Divina: What do you need most from Jesus right now?

"Lord Jesus, send down your Holy Spirit to enlighten my mind to the ways that I may have offended you. Thank you for the Our Father and for teaching us how to pray. Give me a prayerful and forgiving heart that is full of hope, a heart that will never despair or despise. Amen."

"Heavenly Father, I go to my prayer closet on behalf of _____ and pour out my heart to you. You know better than I what _____ needs, and I pray for your will to be done in his/her situation. Amen."

Your Heart Prayer:

_____

_____

_____

_____

_____

_____

_____

_____

_____

_____

_____

_____

_____

_____

_____

_____

_____

_____

_____

CHAPTER SIX

The Remedy of Joy

Jesus is the master of joy; he is its architect and its origin, and without him we can't experience authentic joy. If we only knew with our minds and took into our hearts how much we are loved by God, we would never seek a substitute, and we would be filled with great joy! Joy is more than a feeling; it is an abiding security and a sense of well-being, no matter what is going on in our lives. Joy is the fruit of the Holy Spirit that comes from knowing we are deeply and unconditionally loved.

Jesus said, "I have told you this so that my joy may be in you and your joy may be complete. This is my commandment: love one another as I love you" (John 15:11-12). At first glance, this seems like a simple statement because we all know the Golden Rule. Love certainly brings great joy, but as we all know, it can also bring great sorrow. How can we experience complete joy on a daily basis?

There is a treasure hidden within this commandment, and it is contained in the last four words: "*as I love you.*" We want our loved ones with addictions to know how much they are loved by God. We can communicate that love most clearly through our joy. If our faith and our relationship with Jesus do not bring joy to our lives, then it will not be attractive to anyone who is suffering. As Pope Francis has said, "Sometimes these melancholic Christians' faces have more in common with pickled peppers than the joy of having a beautiful life."[21]

If we are not walking out of Mass and into the world with a smile on our faces or with a sense of peace and quiet joy in our hearts, then we are truly missing something. We owe it to the rest of humanity to bring the miracle of "God with us" into our hurting world. This is our mission!

Communicating our joy and God's love can be as simple as writing a note of encouragement to our loved one or drawing her attention to something that is beautiful in nature. Simple joys revive the heart and breathe life into a troubled soul. Love is most believable when it is offered with no strings attached. Knowing how much we are loved by God helps us to love freely and authentically.

A Daily Commitment

Let's not forget that the enemy of our souls does not want us to know how much we are loved by God. This is his greatest tactic in trying to steal our joy. That's why we have to make a daily commitment to choose joy over our tendencies toward pessimism, negativity, resentment, and fear. Worry, more than anything else, can cause us to lose our joy. St. Paul taught us how to combat this:

> Rejoice in the Lord always. I shall say it again: rejoice! Your kindness should be known to all. The Lord is near. Have no anxiety at all, but in everything, by prayer and petition, with thanksgiving, make your requests known to God. Then the peace of God that surpasses all understanding will guard your hearts and minds in Christ Jesus. (Philippians 4:4-7)

When we make a commitment to joy and release our anxiety through prayer, we have the promise of peace from our

Lord. It's not just ordinary peace but a peace that surpasses all understanding!

I have often used this passage from Psalm 16 as a daily prayer of joy. I like to pray it at night because it settles my mind on God's care and protection as a source of my joy. You can also adapt this prayer by filling in your loved one's name and personalizing it for that person:

> I bless the LORD who gives me counsel;
>> in the night also my heart instructs me.
> I keep the LORD always before me;
>> because he is at my right hand, I shall not be moved.
> Therefore my heart is glad, and my soul rejoices;
>> my body also rests secure.
> For you do not give me up to Sheol,
>> or let your faithful one see the Pit.
> You show me the path of life.
>> In your presence there is fullness of joy;
>> in your right hand are pleasures forevermore.
> (Psalm 16:7-11, NRSV)

A life of addiction is a joyless life filled with fear rather than love. And fear, more than anything else, fuels the addiction. People who are addicted fear a sober life for many reasons. They fear that they will never experience the relief or pseudo-enjoyment they feel when under the influence of their addictive substance or activity. They fear having to deal with the financial, relational, physical, or other consequences of their addictions. They fear being "found out" and rejected by those who discover who they "*really*" are without the addiction. And finally, they are in the double bind of fearing both failure and success at the same time when it comes to quitting an addiction.

As compassionate bystanders, we need to find a way to communicate God's joy to combat all this fear. If God were to write a prescription for joy, it might read like this: "Take two praise pills twice daily for the rest of your life"!

The Power of Praise

Most of us wait to praise God until something really good happens, but that is not what we are instructed to do. This is what St. Paul tells us: "Rejoice always. Pray without ceasing. In all circumstances give thanks, for this is the will of God for you in Christ Jesus. Do not quench the Spirit" (1 Thessalonians 5:16-19).

No matter what our circumstances, we are called to give thanks and praise to God. Why? Because when we pray this way, we unleash the power of the Holy Spirit, which is the power of love, into any situation. These prayers of praise are not celebrating the bad things that are happening but are calling upon the goodness of God to make all things new.

When we are at Mass, we say these powerful words:

Priest: The Lord be with you.
People: And with your spirit.
Priest: Lift up your hearts.
People: We lift them up to the Lord.
Priest: Let us give thanks to the Lord our God.
People: It is right and just.
Priest: It is truly right and just, our duty and our salvation,

always and everywhere to give you thanks,
Father, most holy,
through your beloved Son, Jesus Christ. (Eucharistic Prayer II)

Giving thanks isn't just a good idea—it's our duty and our salvation! The next time you're at Mass, mentally lift up your loved one to the Lord as you say these words and praise and thank him. Placing your loved one into the hands of Jesus during Mass is a powerful way to stir up praise in your heart as you ask the Spirit to help and heal those who suffer with addictions.

Our Holy Helper

1 Thessalonians 5:19 states very plainly, "Do not quench the Spirit." The role of the Holy Spirit is vital in our prayer mission for those who are addicted. The third Person of the Trinity was sent by God to be love in action on earth; he was sent to aid us, to be our counselor, our advocate, and the friend closest to our hearts. In short, the Holy Spirit is on our side when it comes to desiring freedom from the addictions of our loved ones. He is on the front line of the battle.

As prayer warriors, we are called to put on the full armor of God. Our enemy is not just the addiction but the evil one who wants to destroy souls. We are told to

draw your strength from the Lord and from his mighty power.
Put on the armor of God so that you may be able to stand firm
against the tactics of the devil. . . . Stand fast with your loins
girded in truth, clothed with righteousness as a breastplate,

and your feet shod in readiness for the gospel of peace. In all circumstances, hold faith as a shield, to quench all [the] flaming arrows of the evil one. And take the helmet of salvation and the sword of the Spirit, which is the word of God. (Ephesians 6:10-11, 14-17)

When we are armed for the battle and have joy in our hearts, the devil doesn't stand a chance! When we remember that we are not alone, that we and all those who are addicted are infinitely loved by God, and that praise is a powerful force for healing and salvation, we will be able to stay focused on our mission of love, mercy, and hope. Holy Spirit, come!

Week One: Jesus Is Our Joy

Reflection: John 15:9-10

[Jesus said,] "As the Father loves me, so I also love you. Remain in my love. If you keep my commandments, you will remain in my love, just as I have kept my Father's commandments and remain in his love."

Lectio Divina: How will you remain in the love of Jesus this week?

"My dear Lord, help me to love with an authentic love and a genuine joy. Fill me with the knowledge of how much you truly love me so that I can communicate that love to others, especially to my loved one who is addicted. Show me how to appreciate the simple joys as well as the profound ones, and to share them with all those I encounter. Amen."

"Lord, I pray that a desire for your joy and love will pierce _____'s heart and lead him/her to reach out beyond the addiction. Send your Spirit to bring a holy restlessness, even a sense of desperation, if need be, to get _____'s attention, and help me to trust in that process as it unfolds in his/her life. Amen."

Week Two: A Daily Commitment

Reflection: Psalm 51:10, 12 (NRSV)

> Create in me a clean heart, O God,
>   and put a new and right spirit within me. . . .
> Restore to me the joy of your salvation,
>   and sustain in me a willing spirit.

Lectio Divina: What do you need to let go of so that Jesus can restore your joy?

"O sweet and merciful Jesus, I promise to make a decision for joy each day, even when I don't feel like it. Lord, create in me a clean heart, put a right spirit within me, and restore my joy. Amen."

"Dear Lord, day by day I ask you to seek out _____ and keep knocking on the door of his/her heart. Give _____ the courage to let go of the fear and shame that fuel the addiction, and make room in his/her heart for joy. Amen."

Week Three: The Power of Praise

Reflection: Hebrews 13:15

> Through him [then] let us continually offer God a sacrifice of praise, that is, the fruit of lips that confess his name.

Lectio Divina: When you lift up your heart to Jesus, what sacrifice of praise will you offer?

"Dear Jesus, I lift up my heart to you, and I will not despair or compare my life circumstances with others. I will cling to your word and praise your name, no matter how difficult and hopeless things may seem. I promise to take seriously my duty to praise you and thank you with gratitude in my heart. Amen."

"Dear Jesus, I lift up _____ to you and make a vow to give you thanks always and everywhere, to pray without ceasing and offer up a sacrifice of praise on his/her behalf. I trust that you can and will make all things new in _____'s life. Amen."

Week Four: Our Holy Helper

Reflection: Ephesians 6:12, 18

> For our struggle is not with flesh and blood but with the principalities, with the powers, with the world rulers of this present darkness, with the evil spirits in the heavens. . . . With all prayer and supplication, pray at every opportunity in the Spirit.

Lectio Divina: How are you being called to pray in the Spirit for your loved one who is addicted?

"Come, Holy Spirit, equip me with the holy armor of God, and enlighten my heart in your battle for souls. In a special way, I need your aid to be a prayer warrior for _____. Together we will cry out to the Lord for healing, hope, and complete recovery in mind, body, and spirit. Amen."

"Holy Spirit, reveal your power and presence to _____ even in the midst of the addiction. Help _____ to know that you are the friend closest to his/her heart and want only good for his/her soul. Break through the strongholds, and lead _____ into your light. Amen."

Your Heart Prayer:

_____

_____

_____

_____

_____

_____

_____

_____

_____

_____

_____

_____

_____

_____

_____

_____

_____

_____

_____

_____

CHAPTER SEVEN

The Pathway to Peace

There is a simple line in Scripture that offers us a powerful insight when it comes to acceptance of hardship in our lives and in the lives of those we care about:

Beloved, do not be surprised at the fiery ordeal that is taking place among you to test you, as though something strange were happening to you. (1 Peter 4:12, NRSV)

In other words, there is no reason for us to be alarmed, confused, or condemned by our crosses and hardship, because we all have them. This is important since many of us who care for someone who is addicted can stay stuck when we insist on asking the question, "Why?" We agonize over why our loved one is or remains addicted, or we repeatedly wonder, "Why does he want to keep destroying himself?" or "Why does she keep lying to me or using or hurting me or others when she knows she is going to get caught?" We can drive ourselves crazy with these "why" questions!

The first step to accepting the hardship of addiction and all that it involves means letting go of our need to intellectually understand, explain, or otherwise make sense of what is happening to the person who is addicted. Acceptance is really not a matter of the mind but of the heart. If we are going to accept hardship as a pathway to peace, then we will need to do it at the heart level.

Our greatest model for acceptance as a pathway to peace is our Blessed Mother. We are told in Scripture that Mary "treasured all these words and pondered them in her heart" (Luke 2:19, NRSV). Mary's words are few and far between in Scripture and we don't know all the details of her earthly life and experience, but we can glean some things from what we do know. After reflecting on Mary's life and words in Scripture, the Holy Spirit revealed to me a way of pondering that I have shared with many as one way to embrace acceptance and peace in any of life's hardships.

This way of pondering comes in the form of four simple yet profound questions that we can reflect on and take to prayer. These questions can take the place of the ones that swirl around in our hearts regarding the person with the addiction, the ones that never seem to get answered. Instead of going nowhere, these questions are life-giving and bring us further down the path to peace.

Ecce: Behold, I Am the Handmaid of the Lord

Have you ever considered what the word "behold" truly means? The angel Gabriel had already said it two times before Mary responded, and her response was a repetition of this seemingly simple word. But there is more than meets the eye, so to speak, when it comes to the act of beholding.

To behold means to consider something with your mind and in your spirit. It is to observe, not just with your physical sight, but with the eyes of your heart; it is to take something all in, not just with your thoughts, but with your whole being. Mary is indicating with this word "behold" that *she is ready to accept and receive without reservation and with full trust* her role as handmaid. It is a word that reflects Mary's beautiful and holy receptivity, which brings us to our first question to ponder:

What am I being invited to receive through this experience?

Through every difficult circumstance, God wants to give us something good. Through this question, we are asking to receive the often hidden gift that God wants to give us in times of trial. We are being invited to a greater receptivity that is based on a trust that isn't dependent on what we know but on what God knows is best for us and for those we love and care about. Jesus invites us to "Come to me, all you who labor and are burdened, and I will give you rest" (Matthew 11:28).

Many of us wrestle with our burdens and carry them much too long. The truth is that we cannot receive all the goodness that the Lord intends to infuse into our lives if we stay focused on our worries, anxieties, and burdens. First and foremost, Jesus offers us rest.

What else might the Lord want you to receive in this circumstance of praying for someone who is addicted? Could it be that he is trying to teach you something, heal you of something, or give you some piece of wisdom or hope to pass on? Ponder this question as Mary did when she inquired, "How can this be?" (Luke 1:34), and wait for the Lord's response.

Fiat: May It Be Done to Me according to Your Word

When Mary finally understood what God and the Holy Spirit were inviting her to receive, she unreservedly responded with her whole heart and said yes!

Mary did not put conditions on her *fiat*, or yes, to God. She offered herself to him with complete and total generosity. Her example helps us to offer our own yes to God in the midst of the chaos and hardship of addiction. This leads to our next question to ponder:

How will I offer my yes in response?

God invites, and we respond—either with a yes, a no, or a lukewarm, halfhearted effort. We already know through Scripture how God feels about the last option: "Because you are lukewarm, neither hot nor cold, I will spit you out of my mouth" (Revelation 3:16). When the prophet Jonah told God no to his request to go and preach salvation to the Ninevites, he ended up getting spit out of the mouth of a whale!

The response that God deserves from each one of us is a wholehearted yes, just like Mary's. Her simple yes was not focused on the temporal world and its situations or circumstances, nor was it motivated by any desire for personal gain. Mary's yes flowed from the meekness in her heart. Jesus said, "Learn from me, for I am meek and humble of heart"(Matthew 11:29). Meekness is not about being weak but about lacking an inner harshness; a meek heart is one that looks to confirm rather than condemn. A meek heart is always open to the potential good in others; it sees past the present circumstances and affirms that with God all things are possible.

While reflecting on his long life, a wise friend remarked, "My greatest blessings have come from my heaviest burdens." He could never have said that if he had not, over and over again, said yes to God, even in the face of uncertain, difficult, or heartbreaking circumstances. When we say yes to God, his greatness enters the world.

Magnificat: My Soul Proclaims the Greatness of the Lord

Mary's Magnificat, the song of her heart that flowed from her complete yes to Jesus, is a song that we are all invited to sing. Mary said, "My soul proclaims the greatness of the Lord" (Luke 1:46). Some translations read, "My soul magnifies the greatness of the Lord." The word "magnify" gives us the proper perspective for how we are called to deal with any of life's challenges or struggles. In the words of John the Baptist, "He must increase; I must decrease" (John 3:30).

The more we allow God into our troubled situations, the greater we will magnify him, which leads us to our third pondering step:

How will I magnify God to others through the situation?

Stated another way, this question asks, "How are we being called to bring the light and life of Jesus into this present hardship?" In Mary's case, she often did this through her hidden gentleness and silence. Scripture does not reveal what Mary did in most of the situations she encountered in her life, but we know how she responded. In all cases, she magnified God and was a conduit of his will. Through prayer, we can ask her to show us how to fall in love with God's will, no matter what it is, and for her intercession for the grace to carry it out.

Jesus is not only our Savior but also our friend. And as with our friends on earth, the more time we spend with him, the more we listen and learn about his way of doing things, the more likely we are to magnify him. This reminds me of two women I met at a banquet. After sitting down at our table, they quickly volunteered that they were both octogenarians and began happily chatting with everyone. It wasn't long before I noticed that they had almost the same laugh and shared similar mannerisms. They even finished each other's sentences. So I asked, "Are you sisters?"

It turns out that they were not related but had been friends for nearly seventy years! Their closeness had caused them to grow in likeness with one another. This is how it can be with Jesus and us. We can become like him so that others can recognize his greatness through us. Jesus tells us, "You are the light of the world. . . . Just so, your light must shine before others, that they may see your good deeds and glorify your heavenly Father" (Matthew 5:14, 16).

How can the actions that you take toward the person in your life with an addiction bring glory to God? This is not a question that you can answer on your own; it will require some pondering and prayer. Sometimes the answer is not as obvious as you might think. In fact, there are times when the "action" we are called to take is to do nothing at all, and this may be the hardest of all ways for us to magnify the Lord.

Recall that in Scripture, there were times when, in the face of the demanding needs of the crowd, Jesus walked away and went off by himself to pray. For example, Luke writes, "The report about him spread all the more, and great crowds assembled to listen to him and to be cured of their ailments, but he would withdraw to deserted places to pray" (5:15-16).

When Jesus received word that his close friend Lazarus was very sick, the expectation was that he would immediately stop what he was doing and go to Bethany to cure him. He did not. As a result, Lazarus died, and what seemed like the worst possible scenario came to pass. However, with Jesus it wasn't the end of the story, and he raised Lazarus from the dead.

Even when you feel as if the person with the addiction may be "dead" to you, or even if the person has actually succumbed to an addiction, remember that Jesus *always* has the last word, and that word is *mercy*. We are called to pray for the living and the dead. In every case, our prayers will help us to magnify the Lord and help our loved one with an addiction.

Cana: Do Whatever He Tells You

The wedding at Cana (John 2:1-11) is a beautiful illustration of Mary's loving heart and demonstrates the fruit of her pondering. She is there at the wedding feast with a watchful eye, just as she looks down upon us from heaven. When she notices a problem, she goes to Jesus, just as she intercedes for us now. He responds to her promptings, as he always does, and she points us in the right direction, directly to her son. He will tell us what to do.

In her Magnificat, Mary proclaims, "The Mighty One has done great things for me, / and holy is his name" (Luke 1:49). When we do what God tells us to do, we will not only be fulfilled, but we will be bringing about his greatest good in our own life and in the lives of others. Isn't that what we want for the person who is addicted? Isn't that what we want for ourselves?

Instead of focusing and worrying about the problems brought on by the addiction, instead of asking why, we will breathe God's goodness and life into the situation when we seek the answer to this question:

> *What "great things" is God accomplishing in me*
> *or through me in this situation?*

Anytime we return the focus back to God and away from our worries, we are following in the footsteps of Mary on our journey of trust. When we give God the glory, it means that we are no longer letting our problems rule our lives. As my friend Gloria says, "Our problem can become our god." When we acknowledge the "great things" that God is doing in the midst of our pain, we give him permission to work a miracle of mercy in our lives, just as he did at Cana.

Sharing our own personal stories of how Jesus has touched our lives, how he has helped us or healed us, is a powerful way of helping others who are caught up in addiction and feeling very far from him. It's hard for anyone to accuse us of being judgmental (because many active addicts feel judged unjustly) or of proselytizing when we simply share from our hearts the "great things" that God is doing in our own lives or in someone else's life.

These are stories we simply share and then let sink into the heart of another. We plant the seed, and *God* does the rest. We don't have to convert anyone; we just have to share the good news that we've experienced and let those with addictions know that God wants to do the same great thing in their lives too. Remember: God is no respecter of persons. He doesn't play favorites because we are all his favorites, addicted or not.

A True Story

John, whose son struggled with addiction for twenty-five years, wrestled with feelings of tremendous guilt. He felt that as a father, he had fallen short and could have been more understanding of his son as he grew up. John carried around the belief that his own distance and critical nature were the reasons why his son became a drug addict. To try and make up for it, John would often bail his son out of difficult situations caused by the addiction and take on burdens that were the result of his son's lack of responsibility. In many instances, John's guilt was driving him to make decisions that were not as helpful as they could have been for his son or for himself. As a result, John went into debt and his marriage suffered. In short, life became pretty unmanageable for John, and he felt depressed and anxious most of the time.

Through spiritual counseling, John was able to dissect the faulty reasoning that had led to his excessive guilt. Through prayer and pondering, John recognized that his guilt was not helping his son and that it was hurting his relationships with others, especially his relationship with God. Asking the question "What am I being invited to receive through this situation?"

John discovered that God was inviting him to release the burden of his guilt and shame over the way he had parented his son and receive the Lord's peace, mercy, and love. In many ways, John was being invited to take his own "seventh step" in the twelve-step recovery process: to humbly ask God to remove his shortcomings—his excessive guilt.

Through the pondering process, John's next consideration was how to respond to this invitation with a personal yes to the Lord. He had lived with the guilt for so long that he had no idea how to live without it. One day John visited a prayer grotto behind a local church. Later he would call it his "day of reckoning" because it was then that he knelt down and cried out to God to take away his guilt. He also asked for the grace to resist the temptation to take it back. Shortly thereafter, John went to Confession and received absolution.

John felt immediate relief, but he was also not sure what to do next. He took his counselor's suggestion to "let go and let God" take the lead in his relationship with his son. John found that the more he did this, the less he reacted out of a sense of guilt and the more he was able to respond with compassion for his son. While guilt had drawn John down into a rut of resentment and compulsive overdoing for his son, compassion helped him to be clear about what he could and could not do for him. Over time and with practice, John learned how to love and communicate concern for his son without trying to make everything okay when it wasn't. Without realizing it, John was learning how to "magnify the Lord" by letting go of his guilt and showing a proper level of concern for his son.

Finally, through this pondering process, John was able to recognize the action of grace and God's hand in the situation with his son. He was able to grow in trust that God would bring about something good from the addiction even when things were bad. This new level of trust is making a difference in John's relationship with his son, one day at a time, and he is quick to thank God for that.

Week One: Behold, I Am the Handmaid of the Lord

Reflection: Matthew: 11:28-29

"Come to me, all you who labor and are burdened, and I will give you rest. Take my yoke upon you and learn from me."

Lectio Divina: What are your barriers to receiving God's rest?

"Blessed Mother Mary, no matter what happened in your life, you maintained your dignity and a quiet gentleness. Please help me to fall in love with God's will even when it is difficult or hard to bear, and help me to be at peace. Amen."

"Blessed Mother, entrusting my loved one with an addiction to you, I pray that your peace, grace, and intercession will flood his/her life. Help _____ to find rest and comfort in God alone. Amen."

Week Two: May It Be Done to Me according to Your Word

Reflection: Matthew 11:29-30

"I am meek and humble of heart; and you will find rest for yourselves. For my yoke is easy, and my burden light."

Lectio Divina: How will you embrace meekness in your situation/relationship with the person who is addicted?

"Blessed Mother, give me the grace to offer a complete and unconditional yes to God and the action of the Holy Spirit in my life. Let my yes be permission for Jesus to transform my heart so that I might learn from him and be an example of meekness and humility of heart, just like you. Amen."

"O dear Mother, I cry out from the depths of my heart for _____, who has chosen a path that is difficult and destructive. Help him/her find the way back to God's loving embrace and have the humility to say yes to God's mercy and help. Amen."

Week Three: My Soul Proclaims the Greatness of the Lord

Reflection: 2 Thessalonians 1:11-12

> To this end, we always pray for you, that our God may make you worthy of his calling and powerfully bring to fulfillment every good purpose and every effort of faith, that the name of our Lord Jesus may be glorified in you, and you in him, in accord with the grace of our God and Lord Jesus Christ.

Lectio Divina: What things will you do to draw nearer in faith to the Lord this week?

"Blessed Mother, I choose to magnify the Lord in every circumstance, especially in my actions and interactions with the person who is addicted. I beg that the Lord bring about the fulfillment of every good purpose in my life and in the life of _____. Amen."

"Sweet Mother of Mercy, behold your child who is hurting and whose soul is dying! Please bring _____ to the throne of grace so that God may be glorified through his/her healing from addiction. I ask this in Jesus' name. Amen."

Week Four: Do Whatever He Tells You

Reflection: Colossians 3:1-2

> If then you were raised with Christ, seek what is above, where Christ is seated at the right hand of God. Think of what is above, not of what is on earth.

Lectio Divina: Where is your focus?

"O my dear Mother, I trust and believe in your care and concern for my loved one and me. I seek a miracle in my heart and an outpouring of God's grace in my relationship with _____. I am so grateful that you will always be my mother and our perpetual help. Amen."

"Dearest Mary, help _____ to realize that he/she is God's favorite and never outside of his watchful gaze. Help _____ to look up from the pit of his/her addiction toward heaven and to cry out for all the good things that come from above. Amen."

Your Heart Prayer:

_____

_____

_____

_____

_____

_____

_____

_____

_____

_____

_____

_____

_____

_____

_____

_____

_____

_____

_____

_____

_____

Chapter Eight

The Truth Shall Set You Free

As a little girl, I used to take delight in climbing the large weeping willow tree in my backyard. Nestled in the crook of a hideaway branch, I felt as if I were perched on top of a throne, high above the earth. The bird's-eye view captured my imagination as I pretended that the entire neighborhood was my kingdom. From that vantage point, everything looked so much more beautiful and interesting, and I can still remember the exhilaration I felt. I was on top of the world!

As an adult, there have been many times and situations when I wished that I could, even for a few hours, take a "God's-eye view" of my life and look down from on high with a better perspective. Maybe from that angle, things would be clearer or would provide me with a more direct route to where I should go or what I should do. Even as I wish this, I am reminded that Jesus did just the opposite!

A Right Attitude

Jesus had the heavenly view and traded it for an earthly one so that he could walk among us as our Lord, Savior, and friend. In doing so, he experienced our pain, our joys, our temptations, and everything else we humans experience except sin. We are encouraged in Scripture to

> have among yourselves the same attitude that is also yours in
> Christ Jesus,

Who, though he was in the form of God,
did not regard equality with God something to be grasped.
(Philippians 2:5-6)

Let us breathe a little sigh of relief as we embrace the following truth: we are not meant to have all the answers! We
cannot possibly know what is best, so we are simply called to
take this sinful world as it is and leave the rest to Jesus. Jesus
meets each and every one of us just where we are, regardless
of our sin or circumstance.

To help those who are addicted, we need to have "among
ourselves the same attitude as Jesus" and try to meet people
where they are and not where we would like them to be. We
can't help them from a distant high perch of judgment or condemnation. Instead, we are called to walk alongside them with
our prayers and an attitude of "there but for the grace of God
go I." When we accept people who are addicted as they are
and not as we would want them to be, we are performing an
act of love and mercy!

At this point, it is good to remember something that St. Paul
tells us in Philippians 1:6: "I am confident of this, that the one
who began a good work in you will continue to complete it
until the day of Christ Jesus."

Let us claim this Scripture verse on behalf of all who are
addicted and know that God has not abandoned them in their
struggle. Even for those who don't know they need help or
who don't yet want it, God *never gives up* and is always working to bring them further along in their journey toward health
and wholeness.

Five Steps to Freedom

There is a five-step process toward freedom from addiction that everyone must go through in order to fully embrace recovery. It can be an excruciatingly long process for some and a relatively short one for others, with no real way to predict the progress or outcome. There are no shortcuts to the process, however, and no way to circumvent it. Through it, God continues his good work. Sometimes he uses us as instruments of his grace along the way and sometimes he doesn't, but we can always be assured that our prayers make a difference.

As prayer warriors, we can meet the person who is addicted at each one of these steps toward recovery. To restore health and freedom from addiction, a person must

1. Know it.
2. Need it.
3. Feel it.
4. See it.
5. Do it.

Step One—Know It. An addicted person must come to some realization and acknowledgment that he or she has a problem and that the addictive substance or activity is *not helping* to solve it. In this step, a person will become aware on some level or actually come to the conclusion that remaining addicted will be more painful than pursuing recovery.

This is a critical step, and many well-meaning friends and family members bypass it by jumping right into trying to problem-solve to get the person help before the person sees or experiences the value in it. This is like jumping into the car and speeding to the hospital while leaving the patient back at the curb!

This is the time in the relationship with the addict when it is better to ask questions than to have the answers. This will help her reflect upon the reality of the addiction in her life. This is the "How is that working for you?" phase when we simply hold up a mirror so that the addict can see the reflection staring back and become aware of the painful distortion that her life has become.

Step Two—Need It. Once a person realizes that the addiction isn't working for him anymore, he will need enough time and space to experience the emptiness and restlessness that follow. This is crucial, as it creates a vacuum, a hole in the soul, so to speak, and a keen desire and authentic need for something more and better. This time of neediness is good and necessary, but it is something that the addict has been avoiding at all costs.

To this point, the addict's greatest fear has been "What if this emptiness will never be fulfilled?" The addiction has served to paralyze him in that fear. Now faced with his neediness, an addicted person must come to know in his own way and time that there is something greater and outside of himself that will fulfill that need.

He will start to reach out to those around him. Intimacy in friendship is often a new frontier for recovering addicts. Slowly, he will begin to come out of the self-centeredness of addiction and learn how to be vulnerable and intimate in relationships. In essence, he will "wake up" to others. Again, the temptation is for us to step in too quickly and offer substitutes that won't satisfy. We may also rush a relationship with Jesus before he's ready for it, or we may try to fill in the gaps ourselves. Prayer and discernment will help us to remember that the emptiness and holes in our souls were *created* by God, and only he can fill them. He alone knows when and how to fill them.

Our challenge is to allow ourselves to be used by God as *instruments* instead of trying to be the composer and conductor. In this step, what we do is far more important than what we say. The most powerful statement we can make is through how we live our lives and how we put our faith into action. It is more important to show our love for God by loving the best we can. Our example is enough; this is how we become Jesus to others, even if we don't ever mention his name!

Step Three—Feel It. Addiction keeps people in bondage physically, emotionally, and spiritually. In essence, people are stuck and frozen in their pain. While some people are rendered completely numb, with their feelings buried far below the surface, others seem to be overwhelmed with one or another emotion, like rage or despair. Whatever the case, authentic feelings are crippled, and most addicts are afraid of the full impact of their emotions.

A hidden heart cannot be healed, and during this step, the person with the addiction is the most vulnerable. It is hard to feel your feelings when you haven't learned how to or when you haven't felt them for a long time. It takes courage to share this struggle, and the person has to know in her heart of hearts that she will not be rejected because of what and how she feels.

As helpers and pray-ers, we are called to unconditionally accept and suspend all judgment regarding whatever feeling or emotion the person is expressing or experiencing. Have in your mind the image of a turtle that finally gets the courage to poke his head out of his shell after a storm. If he senses that there is any danger at all in the form of judgment or condemnation, he will quickly pull his head back in and hide within that shell, and it may take a long time to coax him back out again. Affirmation is the single greatest gift you can give the person at this time.

Step Four—See It. Once a person begins to experience all the feelings that were hidden and forbidden throughout the addiction, he will become empowered. He will learn that his feelings are not to be feared but can be his "friends" throughout the healing process. Experiencing our emotions gives us the courage to face reality. Once we get clear about what we feel, we can see things rightly, even when what we see may not be pretty.

An addict usually leaves behind a destructive trail. Broken relationships, broken promises, lost dreams and opportunities litter the landscape of the past. For the person who may have accompanied the addict through it all, this destruction is not so easy to ignore or forget. For the addict, it might take a bit of time for this reality to come into focus.

As much as we'd like, we can't force clarity on anyone. We can't make them see what they are not ready or able to see. A person reaches Step Four when he begins the process of taking a serious look at how the addiction has affected his life and the lives of those around him. At this point, the person with the addiction might seek out the Sacrament of Reconciliation. She might need a friend to listen quietly as she reflects on what has happened.

This is a step that requires us to have almost superhuman restraint so that we do not dole out advice or admonition.

A spiritual director or counselor can be of great help for the addicted person at this step, and that might be our most powerful prayer at this time: we can ask God to bring such a person into the life of our friend or loved one.

Step Four is not a "once and done" step. If we are to grow as human beings and in holiness, we will need to revisit this step again and again. It is not just for someone who is approaching recovery but for all of us.

Finally, *Step Five is the "do it"* step because it involves putting all of the other steps into practice to embrace a life that is addiction-free. If a person commits to these steps and applies them, she will experience recovery and freedom.

A Special Devotion

The beautiful Catholic devotion to the Sacred Heart of Jesus can help in the healing of emotions (the addict's as well as our own), and it can also help us to meet the person with the addiction wherever he or she is. Most are familiar with the image of Jesus holding or pointing to his human heart, surrounded by flames and a crown of thorns with a cross at the top. In many of these images, Jesus is literally wearing his heart on his sleeve, an expression that describes those who are honest and open with their emotions.

When Jesus appeared to St. Margaret Mary Alacoque (1647–1690), he came to her and all of humanity in much the same way that the addict does, with an unquenchable thirst for love. Of this encounter, the saint wrote this:

And He showed me that it was His great desire of being loved by men and of withdrawing them from the path of ruin into which Satan hurls such crowds of them, that made Him form the design of manifesting His Heart to men, with all the treasures of love, of mercy, of grace, of sanctification and salvation which it contains, in order that those who desire to render Him and procure for Him all the honor and love possible, might themselves be abundantly enriched with those divine treasures of which this Heart is the source.[22]

The Sacred Heart devotion leads us to an encounter with the heart of Jesus that helps us fall in love with him in a very personal way. We can consecrate ourselves and our loved ones to Jesus' Sacred Heart. Here is the prayer of consecration:

Most Sacred Heart of Jesus, I consecrate myself, my family, my home, everything I have and everything I am, to your service forever. Please protect and bless me, my family, and all those dear to me, especially _____, who is struggling with an addiction.

With this prayer, we can imagine that we are placing our loved ones and those we know who are struggling with addiction into the very heart-wound of Jesus, from where his precious blood flows.

Some families take the devotion a step further and enthrone their homes to the Sacred Heart of Jesus. This involves a period of prayerful preparation and a short yet solemn ceremony during which an image of the Sacred Heart is processed and placed in a prominent spot in the home. The family gathers around the image and proclaims Jesus as the Lord and King of their home and as the central focus of their family life. Far from just placing a picture on the wall, the family invites Jesus into their home as a friend who will always be with them.

St. Margaret Mary explained this devotion further:

> He should be honored under the figure of this Heart of flesh, and its image should be exposed. . . . He promised me that wherever this image should be exposed with a view to showing it special honor, He would pour forth his blessings and graces. This devotion was the last effort of His love that He would grant to men in these latter ages, in order to withdraw them from the empire of Satan which He desired to destroy, and thus to introduce them into the sweet liberty of the rule of His love, which He wished to restore in the hearts of all those who should embrace this devotion. . . . The devotion is so pleasing to Him that He can refuse nothing to those who practice it.[23]

Truth Is a Person

Ultimately, we know that Jesus will be the One who will heal our friend or loved one with an addiction. You may have been praying for a long time for a miracle that has yet to come. While it is rare for an addicted person to be healed instantaneously, it is not impossible, and it's always good to pray for a miracle. As St. Teresa of Avila said, "We pay God a compliment by asking much of him."

Yet as we can see, there is much to pray for along the steps toward healing, and we don't want to miss the potentially slower and more subtle miracles that may be unfolding through them.

Jesus said at the Last Supper as he was preparing to leave his friends, "Do not let your hearts be troubled. You have faith in God; have faith also in me. . . . I am the way and the truth and the life" (John 14:1, 6).

In a world that espouses a multitude of truths and in the midst of addiction where there can be so many lies, we know that there is really only one absolute Truth: the person of Jesus Christ. He came from a mighty throne in heaven to be near us and to save us from ourselves and our sins. At the Last Supper, Jesus showed us the way to life through the Eucharist. It is a comfort to know that when words in prayer fail us, we have the most powerful prayer of all in the holy sacrifice of the Mass.

Jesus comes to each and every one of us where we are at Mass as surely as he came to earth two thousand years ago. It is true that every Mass is a healing Mass, and we have the opportunity, even the obligation, to offer up our Masses for those who need the extra graces from them. This is a powerful and sure way for us to stand in the gap for our loved ones and friends who are addicted. We can claim the promises that flow from the heart of Jesus and take him at his word as he leads us to "know the truth" (John 8:32) that will ultimately set all captives free.

Week One: A Right Attitude

Reflection: Philippians 1:6

> I am confident of this, that the one who began a good work in you will continue to complete it until the day of Christ Jesus.

Lectio Divina: What needs finishing in you?

"Lord, help me to take the world as it is and not how I want it to be. I need your grace to be patient and persevere in my prayers for _____. I trust that you are going to finish the good work that you have begun and that you are leading my loved one on the road to recovery even when I can't see evidence of that. Use me as an instrument of your grace, as you see fit. Amen."

"Lord, I beg you to give _____ a right attitude that will lead to peace in his/her soul and freedom from addiction. Help _____ to see the good work you have started, and plant a desire in his/her heart for a new life in you. Amen."

Week Two: Five Steps to Freedom

Reflection: Hebrews 10:24-25

> We must consider how to rouse one another to love and good works. We should not stay away from our assembly, . . . but encourage one another.

Lectio Divina: How can you speak encouragement into the hearts of others?

"Sweet Jesus, help me to discern how to pray for _____ at each step of the journey toward wholeness and freedom from the addiction. Show me how to be a source of hope, encouragement, and affirmation. Give me the right words to say, but don't let me say too much; help me to be sincere and pure in my motivations. Lord, I need your wisdom and your strength! Amen."

"Lord, give _____ the grace and courage to take the necessary steps toward real recovery and health. Lead him/her to professional help and relationships that will bring about a complete wholeness in mind, body, and spirit. Amen."

Week Three: A Special Devotion

Reflection: Ezekiel 11:19

> I will give them another heart and a new spirit I will put within them. From their bodies I will remove the hearts of stone, and give them hearts of flesh.

Lectio Divina: What turns your heart to stone?

"Lord, I love your adorable and Sacred Heart. Today and always, I consecrate myself and my family to you. Within your heart you carry the wounds of all humanity and the hope of our salvation. Your mercy and love flow from your heart to the whole world. O Jesus, humble of heart, make my heart like yours. Amen."

"O Sacred Heart of Jesus, you died to give _____ a new heart, a new spirit, and a new life. Pour out your mercy and precious blood upon _____. In a special way, I place him/

her in your heart, where he/she will find refuge and strength on this journey toward recovery. Amen"

Week Four: Truth Is a Person

Reflection: Philippians 4:8

> Whatever is true, whatever is honorable, whatever is just, whatever is pure, whatever is lovely, whatever is gracious, if there is any excellence and if there is anything worthy of praise, think about these things.

Lectio Divina: What can you focus on, right now, that is true, just, pure, or lovely?

"Lord, I cling to you and your truth in the midst of my confusion and concern. I know that I can trust in you and that you are always near. Help me to stay positive and focused on whatever is true, honorable, just, pure, lovely, and gracious in my life."

"Lord, I pray that your truth would penetrate the heart of _____ and remove the distortions that occupy his/her mind because of the addiction. Lord, take _____'s every thought captive in obedience to you and your truth (cf. 2 Corinthians 10:5). Amen."

Your Heart Prayer:

_____

_____

_____

_____

_____

_____

_____

_____

_____

_____

_____

_____

_____

_____

_____

_____

_____

_____

_____

_____

CHAPTER NINE

Praying with the Saints

n all difficult times and circumstances, throughout the history of humanity and the Church, God has raised up saints in our midst to help us. They are our sisters and brothers in the body of Christ. They lived lives and encountered hardships that are very similar to our own. When we call upon the saints, we give our prayers an extra boost of intercessory power, and our own faith is bolstered in the process.

These ordinary people were given extraordinary graces and virtues to combat the darkness and trials that surrounded them. Five such individuals come to the forefront as guides on our mission of love, mercy, and hope for those we know who are addicted. They are St. Faustina, Venerable Matt Talbot, St. Monica and St. Augustine, and St. Maximilian Kolbe. Prayers to these saints, as well as suggestions for other special prayers and petitions, are included at the end of the chapter and in the prayer section of this book.

St. Faustina

One of the shortest and surest prayers we can pray is "Jesus, I trust in you." When all other words fail, and even when we falter in our faith, if we proclaim this prayer, it will sustain us and may even change our hearts. Sometimes keeping it simple is the very best way to pray.

Harriet lay awake at night for years waiting for the phone to ring, as she knew somewhere out in the dark of night her daughter was walking the streets to support a heroin addiction. Harriet could not quell the waking nightmares that filled her mind as she imagined the danger her daughter was in. Her sleepless nights had become a way of life. As each dawn arrived with no phone call, her relief was overtaken by the desperate ache she felt in her heart as she faced the empty hole in her life where her daughter used to be.

Trusting in Jesus can be a daily challenge, and there were some days that the only prayer that Harriet could pray consistently was the Divine Mercy Chaplet. This prayer stems from a devotion that Jesus gave to us when he revealed himself to Faustina Kowalska (1905–1938), a Polish religious sister in the Congregation of the Sisters of Our Lady of Mercy. The prayer is associated with the Divine Mercy image, which Jesus asked St. Faustina to have painted. It depicts rays emanating from Jesus' heart, which represent the blood and water that gushed forth from the wound in Jesus' side. Below the image, Jesus asked Faustina to have these words inscribed: "Jesus, I trust in you."

St. Faustina is known as the Apostle of Mercy, and through her writings and this devotion, countless souls have been saved, and many more have come to understand God's infinite mercy for even the most hopeless and hardened sinner.

The Divine Mercy Chaplet is simple yet powerful. Short and direct, it is the perfect prayer to call upon God's mercy for our loved ones and to increase our trust in the Lord at the same time. It is recited on a regular set of rosary beads. Harriet learned to pray the chaplet, and it became her nightly litany. She said the prayer was better than any sleeping pill; through it she discovered that God's love was truly greater, stronger, and mightier than her fears.

Venerable Matt Talbot

Venerable Matt Talbot (1856–1925) is the patron saint of alcoholics. He was one of twelve children born into extreme poverty in the tenements of Dublin, Ireland. His father was a heavy drinker who could not provide for his family, and so he moved them from place to place. As a result, Matt attended formal school only from the ages of eleven to twelve and could not read or write.

When Matt was twelve, he got his first job as a delivery boy for a beer bottling company and also took his first drink. This unhealthy combination seemed to seal his fate. By the time he was sixteen, Matt was a confirmed alcoholic. He was spending all of his money on alcohol and not supporting his family, who remained desperately poor. Matt recalled that he reached his lowest point "when he and his brothers stole a fiddle from a blind street player and sold it for the price of a drink."[24]

While these hardly seem like the actions of a man on his way to sainthood, God had another plan! One fateful Saturday afternoon, after twelve years of hard drinking, Matt found himself without a job, without a drink, and without a friend to help him get one. As he walked home that day, he experienced a moment of immense grace. He suddenly saw with an intense clarity in his mind and heart that he had been wasting his life. At the age of twenty-eight, he saw himself for what he truly was—a fool who had nothing to show for his life.

By the time he reached his home, Matt had made the decision to quit drinking. That very day he walked to Dublin Seminary and made his confession to a priest, who helped him "take the pledge" to renounce alcohol for three months. He returned at six months and then made the pledge for life—but it was not easy! There were no twelve-step programs or counselors or support groups to help him. Nevertheless, Matt maintained sobriety through a recovery program that centered on daily Mass, devotion to the Eucharist, a love for Mary, and spiritual reading. (He learned to read so that he could read the Bible.)

Matt Talbot is often referred to as an "urban ascetic." After his conversion, he lived a life of quiet devotion, holiness, and extreme generosity in spirit and material goods in the midst of the flourishing city life that swirled around him. He offered a pious contrast and example of austerity and charity for those he worked with and those in his neighborhood.

Although there is no cause for sainthood presently open for Matt Talbot's mother, Elizabeth, perhaps there should be! In addition to her husband, all but one of her seven sons were alcoholics. She had no money and barely a roof over her head but managed to remain steadfast in her prayers for her family. She took in work and held out hope that her family could be cured of its problems. Thanks to Matt, she was able to live the last twelve years of her life in relative peace and stability when he moved in to care for her after his father, who never appeared to convert, passed away.

"Never be too hard on the man who can't give up drink," Matt Talbot is often quoted as saying. "It's as hard to give up the drink as it is to raise the dead to life again. But both are possible and even easy for our Lord. We have only to depend on him."

St. Monica and St. Augustine

St. Monica (331–387) was the long-suffering mother of St. Augustine (354–380). In her youth, she was in danger of becoming a "wine bibber," but a stinging rebuke from a maid who found her secretly sipping wine in the wine cellar caused her to stop. Because of this, she is the unofficial patron saint of alcoholics. However, she is known mainly as the patron saint of mothers and married women, and earned that title through decades of praying for the conversion of the hardened hearts of her family members.

The entire family struggled with the chaos of addiction, just like families of today. Monica was a devout Catholic who was given in marriage by her parents to her pagan husband, Patricius. He was difficult and often violent, and also unfaithful. Her mother-in-law, with whom they lived, was a demanding woman who never missed a chance to find fault with Monica. With both of them and three growing children, Monica had her hands full, and no doubt spent many a night on her knees in prayer.

It was through these hard years that Monica grew in patience and perseverance. She clung to God and her faith for solace and strength and prayed for the souls of her husband and mother-in-law. It took twenty years, but both were converted, in part because Monica allowed God to use her as an instrument of peace and gentleness in the home. The greatest challenge for Monica, however, was her son, Augustine.

He was her youngest child and the most brilliant of the three, but he was also lazy and rebellious. Even though Monica had raised Augustine as a Christian, he pursued an active social life that included drinking and a series of affairs and "fast living" that ultimately produced an out-of-wedlock child.

Augustine's keen intellect, coupled with his lack of morals, enabled him to be taken in by the heresy of the day, Manichaeism. It was a philosophy that billed itself as "beyond Christianity" for the smart and sophisticated. In reaction, Monica cut off contact with Augustine, but through a dream she resumed the relationship and followed Augustine to Africa, where she continued to pray for his conversion.

While there, Augustine met and heard St. Ambrose teach and speak. His influence proved genuine, trustworthy, and irresistible, and led to Augustine's conversion at the age of thirty-one. Eventually, Augustine became a priest and bishop of Hippo. His life and writings led to his being canonized and named a Doctor of the Church.

Monica's prayerful had perseverance paid off. Believing that her life's mission was complete with the conversion of her son, she died very shortly after Augustine was baptized.

St. Maximilian Kolbe

St. Maximilian Kolbe (1894–1941) died during World War II in the Auschwitz concentration camp. He had an intense devotion to the Blessed Mother, whom he called "the Immaculata," and a love of Jesus and neighbor that led to his martyrdom. He is the patron saint of drug addicts.

Maximilian was not a drug addict himself but willingly laid down his life for a fellow prisoner by entering the starvation bunker in his place to spare the prisoner's family of the loss of their father and husband. Two weeks of tortuous starvation and dehydration followed. Still, St. Maximilian remained faithful and tended to the needs of the other men. To encourage them, he sang hymns, prayed, and reflected on meditations of Christ's passion.

Trying to make an example out of Fr. Maximilian to scare the others into compliance, his Nazi captors were completely outshined by his heroic virtue and steadfast courage. Even after all the others had died, he remained, praying and peaceful. Finally, the captors injected him with a lethal dose of carbolic acid. He is the patron saint of drug addicts because he was killed by a drug injection.

Pope St. John Paul II proclaimed Maximilian Kolbe the patron saint of the twentieth century. He is also the patron saint of prisoners, families, and the pro-life movement. Many people turn to him as a guardian and protector for their families and, in particular, family members who are in trouble, estranged, or imprisoned, especially by addiction.

You can also engage the help of St. Jude, the patron saint of hopeless causes, or the Confirmation saint of the person you are praying for, if you know it. The archangels St. Michael, St. Gabriel, and St. Raphael are champion intercessors for the cause of addiction. St. Michael is the warrior saint and the one with whom most of us are familiar. St. Gabriel is the messenger and St. Raphael is the healer. You can engage the guardian angel of the person you are praying for and invoke a hedge of protection around that person as he or she struggles with an addiction. It's good to remember that *we are never alone* when we are praying for others.

Week One: St. Faustina

Reflection: Psalm 56:3-4, 5

> O Most High, when I am afraid,
>   in you I place my trust. . . .
> What can mere flesh do to me?

Lectio Divina: What are you most afraid of?

"Dear St. Faustina, help me to trust the will of God in all things and in the healing power of mercy to mend what is broken and restore what seems beyond repair. Amen."

"Dear St. Faustina, I pray for the mercy of the Lord to penetrate the heart of _____ to help him/her to trust in the Lord for all things. May the Lord lead _____ on a journey of trust that will bring him/her back into the arms and grace of God, our loving Father. Amen."

Week Two: Venerable Matt Talbot

Reflection: Psalm 27:13-14

> I believe I shall see the LORD's goodness
>   in the land of the living.
> Wait for the LORD, take courage;
>   be stouthearted, wait for the LORD!

Lectio Divina: Do you believe that you will see recovery for your friend/loved one?

"Lord, I pray that you will help me 'keep it simple,' just as Matt Talbot did in his recovery, staying focused on the basics of our faith to see me through. Give me a childlike love for the Blessed Mother, a belief in the Real Presence, an undivided heart that is generous and pure, and a joy that is nourished by gratitude. Amen."

"Lord, you give us the example of Venerable Matt Talbot as a man who seemed completely lost and beyond your grace. In a single moment, you pierced his heart and changed his mind, leading him back to you. Jesus, I pray for this same conversion and transformation for _____ in your perfect will and timing and for your greater glory. Amen."

Week Three: St. Monica

Reflection: Romans: 12:11-12

Do not grow slack in zeal, be fervent in spirit, serve the Lord. Rejoice in hope, endure in affliction, persevere in prayer.

Lectio Divina: Which of these encouraging suggestions resonates the most with you?

"Dear Jesus, help me to follow the example of St. Monica, who persevered in prayer on behalf of her family and loved ones. When I grow weary and discouraged, lift me up and renew my strength and commitment to pray unceasingly. Blessed Mother, penetrate my heart with your grace, and sustain me with the same hope that sustained you. Amen."

"Dear St. Monica, I pray for your intercession and that of St. Augustine that the right influences penetrate the heart of _____, who is so distracted by the addiction. No matter how strong the sin, no matter how alluring the lifestyle of addiction, let the truth and ways of Jesus become more attractive to _____. Amen."

Week Four: St. Maximilian Kolbe

Reflection: Romans 12:20-21

If your enemy is hungry, feed him; if he is thirsty, give him something to drink; for by so doing you will heap burning coals upon his head. Do not be conquered by evil but conquer evil with good.

Lectio Divina: How do you resist being conquered by evil?

"St. Maximilian, I ask you to give me patience and a compassionate heart toward my enemies and toward the person in my life with an addiction. The evil of addiction can sometimes rear its ugly head, causing hurt, strife, and anger. Let the goodness of God fill my heart, and let it conquer any evil in my life. Amen."

"Lord, I ask you to remove all bitterness, anger, or evil intentions that may be fueled by the addiction in _____'s heart. May St. Maximilian's example of humble yet fierce love and his desire to offer his life for another impress _____ and lead him/her onto a path of virtue and victory over the addiction. Amen."

Your Heart Prayer:

_____

_____

_____

_____

_____

_____

_____

_____

_____

_____

_____

_____

_____

_____

_____

_____

_____

_____

_____

_____

CHAPTER TEN

Letting Go

I f there is a single thread that can help someone whose life is touched by another's addiction, it is the golden thread of surrender. It is the key to our peace and to our relationship with anyone who is struggling with an addiction. And in order to fully surrender the situation and the person to God, we have to learn what it means to "detach with love."

What Is Detachment?

If you are close to someone who is addicted, you could be carrying around a tremendous burden of fear and anxiety over where the addiction will lead. The uncertainty, chaos, and even danger that can occur in the life of someone who is actively using chemicals or engaging in reckless or self-destructive behavior can weigh heavily on those who care for that person. This is when detaching is necessary. But what does that really mean?

Sometimes it is easier to explain detachment by what it doesn't mean. For instance, detaching with love does not mean that we become disinterested or unfeeling; it doesn't mean that we threaten people with withdrawal or cut them off if they don't stop the addictive behavior. In detachment, we may retain a "safe distance" by emotionally or physically stepping back from the intensity of the addiction and the person involved while still allowing a dialogue that shows we care and believe that the person can get clean, get free, and learn from their mistakes. Detachment supports the reality that learning and growing toward recovery are only possible when a person is left to experience and face the consequences of their addiction. In detachment, we guard our hearts for the good of ourselves and for the person who is addicted.

In many ways, I think the phrase should be "detach *for* love" instead of "detach with love" because it is more accurate. When we detach, we make room for love to penetrate and permeate the relationship we have with the person who is addicted. Here's a beautiful poem called "Letting Go," by an anonymous author, that illustrates this point:

> To let go doesn't mean to stop caring: it means I can't do it for someone else.
> To let go is not to cut myself off; it is the realization that I can't control another.
> To let go is not to enable, but to allow learning from natural consequences.
> To let go is to admit powerlessness, which means the outcome is not in my hands.
> To let go is not to try to change or blame another; I can only change myself.
> To let go is not to care for, but to care about.
> To let go is not to fix, but to be supportive.
> To let go is not to judge, but to allow another to be a human being.
> To let go is not to be in the middle arranging outcomes, but to allow others to effect their own outcomes.
> To let go is not to be protective; it is to permit another to face reality.
> To let go is not to deny, but to accept.

To let go is not to nag, scold, or argue, but to search out my
own shortcomings and to correct them.

To let go is not to adjust everything to my desires, but to take
each day as it comes and to cherish the moment.

To let go is not to criticize and regulate anyone, but to try to
become what I dream I can be.

To let go is not to regret the past, but to grow and live for
the future.

To let go is to fear less and love more.[25]

How to Detach

I've spent my entire adult life learning this lesson of surrender and detachment. It's a fluid type of learning process that
incorporates increased awareness, self-knowledge, and spiritual
growth. Learning how to detach with love, if you are having
trouble doing so, is an exercise in grace and is best undertaken
with the assistance of a spiritual director or good counselor
or both. Especially if you are trying to detach from a person
with an active addiction, you should, at the very least, reach
out for the listening ear and caring heart of a faith-filled friend
to keep you accountable.

There are three ways to detach: physically, emotionally, and
spiritually. It's important to remember that any one of these
forms of detachment is not abandonment, even when we put
physical distance between ourselves and the addict. If someone
is exhibiting dangerous, exploitive, or excessively manipula-
tive behavior due to an addiction, just as with other types of
illness, "quarantine" may be in order.

Physical separation and distance are sometimes needed as the appropriate boundaries to ensure that we are safe or treated with respect. An example might be if your spouse is a gambler and your family has no food. This may require that you remove yourself (and your resources) so that you can take care of your needs and those of your children. That is your primary responsibility. In this way, you are detaching with love for your children and the well-being of the family, including your addicted spouse.

Emotional detachment is a little less clear, and it takes a concerted effort, fortified by prayers. In fact, many of the prayers contained in this book will help in the process of emotional detachment. For me, the single most effective aid in detachment and surrender has been my time spent before the Blessed Sacrament in adoration. This habit of silence before the Lord has been all about *his* mysterious love in action upon my heart and my just learning to quietly sit and receive his grace in faith.

Week after week, year after year, I was drawn to sit with Jesus. I visited a basilica in my area that contained a nearly life-sized crucifix and knelt at the foot of it. It was so lifelike that I could look up and see the dirt on Jesus' feet! Most of the time it felt as if nothing was happening, but this is how and where I was ministered to, and it continues to be where my heart and soul are healed.

In those hours, Jesus taught me proper attachment with *him* so that I could disentangle myself from dysfunctional relationships with the addicts in my life. Even if you are not emotionally entangled with someone who is addicted, going to Jesus in the Blessed Sacrament for purification and a deeper experience of the attachment you have with him will make you more effective in your attempts to help anyone with an addiction.

Spiritual detachment is the greatest experience of freedom we can have this side of heaven, yet it can be easily misunderstood. Spiritual detachment does not mean that we extinguish all our desires! Our desires come from God and are necessary to give our lives meaning, purpose, and depth. When we detach spiritually, we embrace a state of internal surrender and a poverty of spirit that help us seek fulfillment only in and through the things of God, not in disordered thoughts, inclinations, or relationships.

The beatitude "Blessed are the poor in spirit, / for theirs is the kingdom of heaven" (Matthew 5:3) states clearly that a detachment of spirit here on earth is like living in heaven! For most of us, this might seem impossible, *but it is not!* Spiritual detachment flows out of our efforts at emotional detachment in concert with Christ, who will show us the way.

What to Detach From

St. Thérèse of Lisieux wrote, "Do all in your power to detach your heart from earthly cares, especially from creatures; then be assured Our Lord will do the rest."[26] Thérèse is talking about our inclinations toward vanity and an inordinate desire to please and look good in front of others at the expense of our relationship with God. An addiction can feed into these tendencies and distort our well-meaning helping relationship with the addict, causing us to place more of our attention and energy on the person than on God.

Self-forgetfulness is the antidote to this tendency, and is aided by our efforts toward detachment. Here is a short list of things to detach from that will set us on the course of self-forgetfulness:

- Guilt over things that are not your fault
- Trying to make everyone happy
- Finding a solution to someone else's problem
- Worry and fear
- Anger
- Taking offense
- Your own version of how things should be

Since there are seven conditions on the list, you may want to choose one for each day of the week to focus on and detach from. As we let go of these conditions that have the potential to derail us, we open ourselves up to God's way of loving others through us.

The Fruit of Detachment

When we watch our loved ones and friends deteriorate or destroy their lives because of an addiction, the very last thing we are inclined to do is detach. Even though it is counterintuitive, detaching with love is an essential survival skill for you and for the person you know who is addicted. St. Paul even suggests that it is a life-and-death decision when he said in his letter to the Romans,

> For those who live according to the flesh are concerned with the things of the flesh, but those who live according to the spirit

with the things of the spirit. The concern of the flesh is death, but the concern of the spirit is life and peace. (8:5-6)

Our efforts toward surrender and detachment are *of the Spirit* and will bring life into the situation of addiction for ourselves and for the one who is struggling with the addiction. Ultimately, the fruit of the Spirit that blossoms through detachment is peace. Sometimes we forget that through Baptism and Confirmation, the fruit of the Holy Spirit is *within us*. This peace is not something we grasp at or attempt to possess as something outside of ourselves; it is something that we allow to take root within us with the help of the Holy Spirit.

Imagine: peace is a fruit that can blossom in our hearts when we learn to detach with love. That is a peace worth cultivating and praying for, both for ourselves and for those who are addicted.

Week One: What Is Detachment?

Reflection: Proverbs 3:5-7

> Trust in the LORD with all your heart,
> on your own intelligence do not rely;
> In all your ways be mindful of him,
> and he will make straight your paths.
> Do not be wise in your own eyes.

Lectio Divina: What personal opinions, thoughts, ideas, or understandings might be helpful for you to detach from?

"Lord Jesus, I know that sometimes I think I know best for others. It is hard for me to let go of my point of view. There are many things and thoughts that I can detach from. Give me the grace to do so. It is such a comforting truth to know that you know the way that my loved ones and I should go. Help me to learn the lesson of detachment. Amen."

"Lord, I know that _____ may not understand and may even perceive my need to detach with and for love as a personal rejection. Help me to detach anyway. Help me to let go of my own understanding and cling to your promises for _____. May he/she do the same. Amen."

Week Two: How to Detach

Reflection: Isaiah 43:18-19

> Remember not the events of the past,
>   the things of long ago consider not;
> See, I am doing something new!
>   Now it springs forth, do you not perceive it?
> In the wilderness I make a way,
>   in the wasteland, rivers.

Lectio Divina: What new thing do you need Jesus to be doing in your life? What "wasteland" needs to be watered?

"Lord, I seek healing in the attachments of my heart and in my personal relationship with others, especially with the person who is addicted. Please make all things new that are meant to be restored, and sever what is broken that should not be restored. Your timing, your wisdom, and your love are all that is needed to help me embrace the promises of new life and refreshment that detachment brings. Amen."

"Dear Jesus, please take care of _____. I trust that your ways are better than my ways to bring _____ to wholeness and a life without the addiction. Let the wasteland of _____'s current situation be made new by your grace. Amen."

Week Three: What to Detach From

Reflection: Matthew 6:33, 34

"Seek first the kingdom [of God] and his righteousness. . . . Do not worry about tomorrow; tomorrow will take care of itself."

Lectio Divina: What do you need to detach from so that you can seek God first?

"Lord, I want to put you first in my life. So many distractions, emotions, and entanglements get in the way. Purify my motives, sanctify my actions, and provide me with the grace to commit to the work of detachment every day. Amen."

"Jesus, please minister to the heart of _____ and take away the anxieties that plague him/her. Right now _____ is living a disordered life, but I know that your love and care for him/her is steadfast, true, and unchanging. Help _____ to catch a glimpse of and an experience of that love. Place a growing desire in his/her heart to seek you above everything else. Amen."

Week Four: The Fruit of Detachment

Reflection: 1 Peter 5:7, 10

> Cast all your worries upon him because he cares for you. . . . The God of all grace . . . will himself restore, confirm, strengthen, and establish you.

Lectio Divina: How can you detach from your worries on a daily basis?

"Dear Lord, I know that worry quenches the Spirit and that your perfect love drives out fear. Today and every day, I cast worry and fear aside to receive the blessings that detachment brings. I welcome the Holy Spirit to let the fruit of peace grow in my heart. In a special way, I cry out to Mary, my Mother, to assist me and to help me follow her example of holy detachment. Amen."

"Jesus and Mary, I commit _____ to your Sacred and Immaculate Hearts. Please restore, confirm, strengthen, and establish him/her as I detach in love and trust in your grace. Amen."

Your Heart Prayer:

_____

_____

_____

_____

_____

_____

_____

_____

_____

_____

_____

_____

_____

_____

_____

_____

_____

_____

_____

_____

_____

_____

_____

_____

CHAPTER ELEVEN

Keeping the Faith

Have you ever heard of this saying: "Prayer is the key to heaven, but faith unlocks the door"? Prayer, learning to detach with love, and all the other knowledge and skills you are putting into practice will make the way for you to receive the precious gift of a deep and abiding faith in Jesus to care for and lead your loved one to recovery.

Such faith is an essential ingredient in our mission to minister and pray for others who are addicted. Scripture defines faith as "the realization of what is hoped for and evidence of things not seen" (Hebrews 11:1). Let's unpack that a bit.

Things Not Seen

You may be surprised to learn that Bill Wilson, the cofounder of Alcoholics Anonymous, was hospitalized for treatment four times and was considered by his family and friends to be a hopeless alcoholic. Yet he spent the last thirty-seven years of his life sober. According to Jeff VanVonderen, an author and speaker who conducts interventions with addicts, it takes an average of fifty-four confrontations before a person realizes that he or she has a problem. "This means that there is hope, that people eventually come to the realization they need help. It means that one person does not carry the entire burden of helping someone realize the problem and that each individual step or effort is not wasted, even if it appears so at the time."[27]

It's tempting to give up when all that we see is the same old addiction on the outside and a seemingly hopeless cycle of false starts when it comes to recovery for our loved one. But none of us can see what is happening or how God is putting our prayers to work below the surface, or at the heart level, for the person who is addicted. Recovery is an "inside job" and ultimately a spiritual battle for the soul of the individual who is addicted. That is why it is so important that we "walk by faith, not by sight" (2 Corinthians 5:7).

More on Faith

According to the *Catechism of the Catholic Church*, "Faith is first of all a personal adherence of man to God" (150). In other words, faith leads us to cling to the truths, words, and works of God and believe in them with our whole hearts, minds, and souls. Faith, the *Catechism* also explains, is a "gift of God, a supernatural virtue infused by him" (153).

So when we find that we are faltering in faith and belief in God's intentions for the healing of our loved one or friend, we can call upon him for a "faith infusion," or transfusion, if you will! We can't force ourselves to have faith, but we can seek God's gift of faith and know that he will honor our request. Like the man who asked Jesus to heal his dying son, we can cry out, "I do believe, help my unbelief" (Mark 9:24).

Got Faith?

Many times in Scripture, after people approach Jesus for help or healing and he heals them, he tells them that their faith has saved them or made them well. One such instance stands out: the story of the four men who carried their friend on a mat because he was paralyzed and could not approach Jesus on his own (Mark 2:1-12).

As they came upon the house in which Jesus was speaking, they noticed that a large crowd had gathered around the door, which prevented them from getting close to him. Undaunted, the four friends proceeded to climb up on the roof, cut through it, and let down the mat on which their ailing friend was lying. Beyond the perseverance of these friends, Jesus "saw their faith" (Mark 2:5) and forgave the sins of the paralyzed man and then healed him. For those of us who are on this prayer journey for our loved ones who are addicted, *we* are those four friends.

We carry our loved ones and friends paralyzed by addiction into Jesus' presence by our prayers as well as our sacrifices and love offerings. We can't make an addict give up an addiction, no matter how hard we might try, but we can persist in our prayers as an act of faith.

Faith in Action

One powerful way to put our faith in action is to apply scriptural affirmations to the addiction situation. The *Catechism of the Catholic Church* says that faith "is founded on the very word of God who cannot lie" and that "to live, grow, and persevere in the faith until the end we must nourish it with the word of God" (157; 162).

Praying with Scripture and claiming scriptural promises plant the beauty of truth in the garden of weeds that has been sown through the lies of addiction. When the word of God takes root in our hearts and our lives, faith grows and love blooms. Here are a few passages that can be adapted by inserting the name(s) of those you are praying for.

The LORD is God from of old,
   creator of the ends of the earth.
He does not faint or grow weary,
   and his knowledge is beyond scrutiny.
He gives power to the faint,
   abundant strength to the weak, [especially _____].
 Though young men faint and grow weary,
   and youths stagger and fall,
They that hope in the LORD will renew their strength,
   _____ will soar on eagles' wings;
   _____ will run and not grow weary,
   walk and not grow faint. (Isaiah 40:28-31)

_____ has peace with God through our Lord Jesus Christ, through whom we have gained access [by faith] to this grace in which we stand, and we boast in hope of the glory of God . . . because the love of God has been poured out into _____'s heart through the holy Spirit. . . . God proves his love for _____ in that while we were still sinners Christ died for us. How much more then, since we are now justified by his blood, will _____ be saved through him from the wrath. (Romans 5:1-2, 5, 8-9)

We do not cease praying for _____ and asking that _____ may be filled with the knowledge of [God's] will through all spiritual wisdom and understanding to live in a manner worthy of the Lord, so as to be fully pleasing, in every good work bearing fruit and growing in the knowledge of God, strengthened with every power, in accord with his glorious might, for all endurance and patience, with joy giving thanks to the Father, who has made _____ fit to share in the inheritance of the holy ones in light. (cf. Colossians 1:9-12)

There is life in the word of God, and when we speak it, we are offering the gift of our faith on behalf of our friends and loved ones who cannot claim it for themselves. This is a work of mercy and a powerful way to pray for them as well.

Week One: Things Not Seen

Reflection: Galatians 6:9

Let us not grow tired of doing good, for in due time we shall reap our harvest, if we do not give up.

Lectio Divina: What seeds are you sowing? What will be your harvest?

"O my Jesus, you fell three times on the road to the cross, and to all who were watching, it appeared to be the ultimate defeat. But God had another plan! Give me the strength to keep the faith and keep praying even when I can see no evidence of change in _____. Help me to keep sowing seeds of prayer and to hold on to hope for the harvest time. Amen."

"Lord, help _____ to not get discouraged on the road to freedom and recovery from addiction. Help _____ to find solace in your assurance that each and every attempt gets them that much closer to the life they long for. There is never failure in falling down, just in not getting back up to try again. Amen."

Week Two: More on Faith

Reflection: Ephesians 2:8

> For by grace you have been saved through faith, and this is not from you; it is the gift of God.

Lectio Divina: How will you thank God for the gift of your faith?

"Lord, send me a 'faith transfusion'! I need the gift of faith to see me through the difficult times and trials brought into my life because of addiction. I know by faith that our greatest trials can lead us to our deepest joys when we cling to your light in the darkness. Amen."

"Dear Jesus, by your grace I ask you to save _____ from addiction. Fill him/her with a longing to seek your light in the darkness and your freedom from the pain and pit of despair. Amen."

Week Three: Got Faith?

Reflection: Romans 10:11

No one who believes in him will be put to shame.

Lectio Divina: What are ways you can nourish your faith this week?

"Lord, let me wear my faith like a badge of honor, just as the four friends did in the story of the paralytic. I believe in your love and in your healing power, and I will keep praying until _____ is released from the bonds of addiction. Alleluia!"

"Lord, right now _____ is paralyzed by the addiction, but I know that you can break those chains! Infuse _____ with a supernatural and unshakable faith in your power to set him/her free. Amen."

Week Four: Faith in Action

Reflection: Hebrews 4:12

Indeed, the word of God is living and effective, sharper than any two-edged sword, penetrating even between soul and spirit, joints and marrow, and able to discern reflections and thoughts of the heart.

Lectio Divina: What Scripture verse speaks life into you?

"Heavenly Father, your Word became flesh and dwelt among us. I claim your word and apply it to my life to lift up my soul and the souls of those for whom I pray. Thank you, Father, for always speaking to our hearts through the Holy Spirit. I am listening! Amen."

"Lord, speak your word into _____'s heart so that he/she may be transformed. May the two-edged sword of your truth sever the bond of addiction and set _____ free. Amen. "

Your Heart Prayer:

_____

_____

_____

_____

_____

_____

_____

_____

_____

_____

_____

_____

_____

CHAPTER TWELVE

Passing It On

You might wonder if there are any hidden blessings or silver linings to the dilemma of addiction. As someone who has been on both sides, as a child of an alcoholic and as an alcoholic who is in recovery, I can wholeheartedly and unreservedly proclaim YES! St. James described the mystery of these hidden gifts when he wrote, "Consider it all joy, my brothers, when you encounter various trials, for you know that the testing of your faith produces perseverance. And let perseverance be perfect, so that you may be perfect and complete, lacking in nothing" (1:2-4).

His Forever Promise

Truly, God meets all of our needs and completes and perfects us in our difficulties. Our hope is not in ourselves or in the things of this earth but in Jesus, our suffering friend who knows what it is like to be human and hurting. As Jesus said to St. Paul when he asked him three times to remove a certain affliction, "My grace is sufficient for you, for power is made perfect in weakness" (2 Corinthians 12:9).

Therefore, we should never be ashamed of our afflictions or weaknesses or of those that plague our friends and loved ones who are addicted. For it is in our relationship with those who are addicted that God's great and saving power shines through.

Our mission of love, mercy, and hope opens the door to life-giving opportunities, both for ourselves and for those for whom we pray. It makes it possible to learn how to receive and give mercy, to experience the authentic freedom of true forgiveness, and to enter into the redeeming love of Jesus Christ. This mission is what Jesus meant when he said, "I came so that they might have life and have it more abundantly" (John 10:10).

Bearers of Hope

While in Rio de Janiero in 2013 for World Youth Day, Pope Francis visited a hospital for the opening of a new wing dedicated to the treatment of drug abusers. He called it a "shrine of human suffering," and spoke to the addicts openly and affectionately, as he always does. When he turned to volunteers and to family and friends, he said this:

> We all need to look upon one another with the loving eyes of Christ, and to learn to embrace those in need, in order to show our closeness, affection and love. To embrace someone is not enough, however. We must hold the hand of the one . . . who has fallen into the darkness of dependency . . . and we must say to him or her: You can get up, you can stand up. It is difficult but it is possible if you want to. . . . I say to us all: Let us not rob others of hope, let us become bearers of hope![28]

I can think of no more worthy vocation, can you?

Love Changes Things

As I was working on the last chapter of this book, I stumbled across this insight from Franciscan priest and author Fr. Jude

Winkler. It seems to perfectly sum up the entire message of what I have been sharing with you.

> Prayers are God-filled words in which our love and God's love are joined. That love embraces the people for whom we are praying, and *love always changes people and situations*. This doesn't mean that we will always get what we want, but Jesus does promise that we will get what we need. (emphasis added) [29]

What an awesome and beautiful promise that we have from our Lord: that we will get what we need! Could it be that we might simply pray, "Lord, help _____ get what he or she needs"? May we completely trust that our love, joined with God's, will embrace those for whom we pray and change their situation for the good, for the better, for the best!

Passing It On

The twelfth step of most self-help recovery programs reads something like this:

> Having had a spiritual awakening as the result of these steps, we tried to carry the message to others and to practice these principles in all of our affairs.

This is the beauty that rises from the ashes of addiction. We claim the grace that Christ offers us, and we pass it on by sharing how his mercy and love can "set the captives free" (cf. Luke 4:18). I'll leave you with an image and the story of a woman who, in the face of great suffering, offered a humble but loving gesture and was rewarded with a tremendous gift and blessing that was imprinted on her heart. She carried that image with her always, and then spent the rest of her life sharing that blessing with others. Her name was Veronica.

She hears the commotion in the streets, and a combination of curiosity and sorrow overwhelms her. The crowd is rowdy, but something deep within her spurs her on. She knows the Rabboni, for she had touched his garment and was made well from the issue of blood. He is truly the Messiah, so why is he now being condemned to die? Her heart races at the thought, and as she catches a glimpse of his battered body, she can barely take a breath.

The throng pushes her, nearly knocking her down. As Jesus trudges up the hill with the heavy cross, Veronica can see his mother, Mary, following him, her face pale and eyes glistening but her steps resolute. A man is suddenly pulled from the jeering crowd to help Jesus; he is reluctant and afraid. But Jesus has already fallen once from the heavy weight of the wooden cross. He is barely recognizable from the brutal scourging he has endured. His bruised and bloodied face is covered with spittle and dirt. With every fiber of her being, Veronica wants to run away from the sight of him, but she doesn't.

Instead, a quiet calm overtakes her and compassion grips her heart. In the midst of the raging spectacle of suffering and evil, she lunges through the sea of people, once again risking everything to get close to Jesus. She reaches out and wipes his holy face with her own tattered garment. As she does, she looks into his eyes and sees only love.

The story of Veronica is our story; it is for all of us who love and care for those who are bearing the heavy cross of addiction. Our prayers are the means by which we can alleviate their suffering. Like Veronica, when we take the risk of compassion, we receive a great reward: the beautiful imprint of Christ upon our hearts. It is that imprint that becomes the hope and healing that others need. It is the message of mercy they are longing to hear. And it is a message worth repeating. Pass it on.

Week One: His Forever Promise

Reflection: James 1:2-4

Consider it all joy, my brothers, when you encounter various trials, for you know that the testing of your faith produces perseverance. And let perseverance be perfect, so that you may be perfect and complete, lacking in nothing.

Lectio Divina: How will you embrace joy through your trials this week?

"My dear Lord, I 'consider it all joy' to experience this trial of addiction in _____'s life. I trust that you will use it to draw me deeper into your loving embrace, strengthen my faith, and make me strong in spirit. Amen."

"Lord, your promises are true and your word is just. Holy Spirit, breathe your life into _____'s heart and fill him/

her with your freedom, forgiveness, and love. May your abundance be enough to satisfy every desire. Amen."

Week Two: Bearers of Hope

Reflection: 1 Peter 3:15-16

Always be ready to give an explanation to anyone who asks you for a reason for your hope, but do it with gentleness and reverence.

Lectio Divina: If someone asks, how will you respond?

"O Jesus, help me to look at _____ with your eyes and to love him/her with your heart. When I am despairing, lift me up; when I am angry, calm my soul. Help me be a bearer of hope in the face of addiction and pain. Amen."

"Heavenly Father, I beg you to send bearers of hope to _____, who is so in need of it. Addiction has robbed him/her of every shred of dignity, every ounce of strength, and every hope of consolation. Give _____ the eyes to see and the ears to hear the good news, and put messengers of it in his/her path. Amen."

Week Three: Love Changes Things

Reflection: 1 Corinthians 13:4-7

> Love is patient, love is kind. It is not jealous, [love] is not pompous,
> it is not inflated, it is not rude, it does not seek its own interests,
> it is not quick-tempered, it does not brood over injury, it does
> not rejoice over wrongdoing but rejoices with the truth. It bears
> all things, believes all things, hopes all things, endures all things.

Lectio Divina: Replace the words "love" and "it" with your
name, and repeat it often throughout the week.

"Lord, help me to love _____ as you do, with patience
and kindness. I do not want to brood over injuries; instead, I
want to rejoice in your truth. I believe that your love endures
forever. Give me the grace to love _____ with your own
love. Amen."

"Lord, I join my love to yours in this quest to save _____
from addiction. I know you are the Savior, and I believe that
your love can transform lives. Help _____ get whatever
he/she needs at this present moment. Amen."

Week Four: Passing It On

Reflection: Matthew 25:40

[Jesus said,] "Amen, I say to you, whatever you did for one of these least brothers of mine, you did for me."

Lectio Divina: Reflect upon the fact that every person with an addiction is Jesus in disguise.

"Lord, continually awaken my spirit to the misery of others, especially those who are addicted, and guide me to see them as you do. Give me the courage to come face-to-face with their suffering without losing myself and all the grace and wisdom I need to be an instrument of your love, mercy, and hope. Amen."

"I rejoice, Lord, in the journey of my life and the life of _____. All is gift; all is grace. I humbly and earnestly ask you, Lord, to bless _____ and keep him/her in the shadow of your wings. Let your face shine upon _____ and be gracious onto _____! Please look kindly upon _____ and give him/her peace. Amen."

Your Heart Prayer:

_____

_____

_____

_____

_____

_____

_____

_____

_____

_____

_____

_____

_____

_____

_____

_____

_____

_____

_____

Prayers

Here are a collection of prayers that will supplement the others in this book, including prayers to patron saints and prayers for special circumstances. I have also included several prayers that have helped me on my journey of recovery with the addicted persons in my life. Finally, I have included a link to a liturgical blessing offered by the Church that may be performed by a priest or layperson.

The Chaplet of Divine Mercy

St. Faustina was taught this prayer in one of her visions, which uses ordinary rosary beads. Here is how to pray it:

1. Make the Sign of the Cross, and then on the first bead, pray

> O Blood and Water, which gushed forth from the Heart of Jesus as a fountain of mercy for us, I trust in You! (Repeat three times.)

You can also pray this optional opening prayer, taken from her diary:

> You expired, Jesus, but the source of life gushed forth for souls, and the ocean of mercy opened up for the whole world. O Fount of Life, unfathomable Divine Mercy, envelop the whole world and empty Yourself out upon us.

2. Pray an Our Father, a Hail Mary, and the Apostle's Creed on the next three beads.

3. Then on the Our Father beads, pray the following:

    Eternal Father, I offer You the Body and Blood, Soul and Divinity of Your dearly beloved Son, Our Lord Jesus Christ, in atonement for our sins and those of the whole world.

4. On the ten Hail Mary beads, pray the following:

    For the sake of His sorrowful Passion, have mercy on us and on the whole world.

5. After all five decades, conclude by saying the following three times:

    Holy God, Holy Mighty One, Holy Immortal One, have mercy on us and on the whole world.

6. You can also add this optional closing prayer:

    Eternal God, in whom mercy is endless and the treasury of compassion inexhaustible, look kindly upon us and increase Your mercy in us, that in difficult moments we might not despair nor become despondent, but with great confidence submit ourselves to Your holy will, which is Love and Mercy itself.[30]

Venerable Matt Talbot

Here is a novena to Matt Talbot for alcoholics. It can be prayed for nine consecutive days for anyone who is addicted, whether to alcohol or some other substance or behavior.

God of mercy, we bless you in the name of your Son, Jesus Christ, who ministered to all who come to Him. Give your strength to _____, who is bound by the chains of addiction. Enfold him/her in your love and restore him/her to freedom through your grace.

Lord, look with compassion on all those who have lost their health and have broken relationships because of their attachment to the object of their addiction. Restore to them the assurance of your unfailing mercy, and strengthen them in the work of recovery. To those who care for them, grant patient understanding and a love that perseveres.

Lord, in your servant Venerable Matt Talbot, you have given us a wonderful example of triumph over addiction, of devotion to duty, and of lifelong reverence of the Holy Eucharist. May his life of prayer and penance give _____ the courage to take up his/her cross and follow in the footsteps of Our Lord and Savior, Jesus Christ. Father, we ask this through Christ our Lord. Amen.[31]

St. Monica

Below is a prayer and a novena to St. Monica.

Dear St. Monica, troubled wife and mother, many sorrows pierced your heart during your lifetime. Yet you never despaired or lost faith. With confidence, persistence, and profound faith, you prayed daily for the conversion of your beloved husband, Patricius, and your beloved son, Augustine; your prayers were answered. Grant me that same fortitude, patience, and trust in the Lord. Intercede for me, dear St. Monica, that God may favorably hear my plea for (mention request here) and grant me the grace to accept his will in all things. Through Jesus Christ, our Lord, in the unity of the Holy Spirit, one God, forever and ever.

God of mercy, comforter of those in sorrow, the tears of St. Monica moved you to convert her son St. Augustine to the faith of Christ. By their prayers, help us to turn from our sins and to find your loving forgiveness. Grant this through our Lord Jesus Christ, your Son, who lives and reigns with you and the Holy Spirit, one God, forever and ever. Amen.[32]

Dear St. Monica, you were once the mournful mother of a prodigal son. Your faithfulness to prayer brought you and your son so close to God that you are now with him in eternity. By your intercession and God's grace, your son St. Augustine became a great and venerable saint of the Church. Please take my request to God with the same fervor and persistence with which you prayed for your own son. (Mention your intention here.)

With your needs, worries, and anxieties, you threw yourself on the mercy and providence of God. Through sorrow and pain, you constantly devoted yourself to God. Pray for me that I might join you in such a deep faith in God's goodness and mercy.

Above all, dear St. Monica, pray for me that I may, like your son, turn from my sin and become a great saint for the glory of God.[33]

St. Maximilian Kolbe

This prayer to St. Maximilian Kolbe is for a friend or family member addicted to drugs.

St. Maximilian Maria Kolbe, your life of love and labor for souls was sacrificed amid the horrors of a concentration camp and hastened to its end by an injection of a deadly drug.

Look with compassion upon _____, who is now entrapped in addiction to drugs and whom we now recommend to your powerful intercession.

Having offered your own life to preserve that of a family man, we turn to you with trust, confident that you will understand and help.

Obtain for us the grace never to withhold our love and understanding, nor to fail in persevering prayer that the enslaving bonds of addiction may be broken and that full health and freedom may be restored to him/her whom we love.

We will never cease to be grateful to God who has helped us and heard your prayer for us. Amen. [34]

St. Jude

St. Jude is the patron saint of hopeless causes. Here is a prayer for his intercession for those who are addicted.

God of life, you made me in your perfect image, to live in your love and to give you glory, honor, and praise. Open my heart to your healing power. Come, Lord Jesus, calm my soul just as you whispered "Peace" to the stormy sea. St. Jude, most holy apostle, in my need I reach out to you. I beg you to intercede for me that I may find strength to overcome my illness. Bless all those who struggle with addiction. Touch them, heal them, and reassure them of the Father's constant love. Remain at my side, St. Jude, to chase away all evil temptations, fears, and doubts. May the quiet assurance of your loving presence illuminate the darkness in my heart and bring lasting peace. Amen.[35]

Prayer to the Archangels

The archangels are powerful intercessors. Here is a prayer to all three archangels for recovery.

Heavenly King, you have given us archangels
to assist us during our pilgrimage on earth.
St. Michael is our protector;
I ask him to come to my aid (and the aid of _____).
Fight for all my loved ones,
and protect us from danger.

St. Gabriel is a messenger of the Good News;
I ask him to help me (and _____)
To clearly hear your voice
and teach us the truth.

St. Raphael is the healing angel.
I ask him to take my need for healing
and that of everyone I know (especially _____).
Lift it up to your throne of grace
and deliver back to us the gift of recovery.

Help us, O Lord,
to realize more fully the reality of the archangels
and their desire to serve us.
Holy angels, pray for us.
Amen.[36]

Prayer for Purity of Mind and Body

Dear God, you have given us a body to keep pure and clean
and healthy for your service and eternal happiness. Forgive
_____ for all unfaithfulness in this great responsibility.
Forgive _____ for every disordered use that _____
has made of your gifts in thought, word, or deed since his/her
rebirth as your own adopted child in Baptism.

Create in _____ a clean heart, O God, and give a
steadfast will, that _____ may be strong for others. Teach
_____ to respect his/her body and the bodies of his/her
fellow creatures. Help _____ to see the glory of perfect
manhood in Jesus Christ and of perfect womanhood in Mary

Immaculate. Inspire _____ with such love for the ideals for which our Savior lived and died that all passions and energies will be caught up into the enthusiasm of his service, and evil things will lose their power. May _____'s body be the servant of his/her soul, and may both body and soul be your servants. Through Christ our Lord. Amen.[37]

Divine Mercy Prayer for a Release from Addiction

This prayer is from the *Handbook of Devotion to the Divine Mercy* and calls on the divine mercy and blood of Jesus.

Lord Jesus, I put myself into your hands this day. I ask you, with all my heart, to cure the terrible addiction to alcohol [or drugs] in _____. Create in them an intolerance for alcohol [or drugs] that will prevent them ever offending those who love them again. And grant [me and all of] their loved ones the grace to forgive them for all the hurt they have caused. Through the Divine Mercy and Blood of Jesus, I also pray that _____ will be healed of all withdrawal symptoms of this terrible affliction. I sincerely ask this in the name of Jesus. Amen.[38]

Prayer for Those Who Have Relapsed

This prayer is taken from *The 12 Step Prayer Book*.

O God of all mercies and comfort, who helps us in times of need, we humbly ask you to behold, visit, and relieve those whom have relapsed [especially_____] for whom our prayers are desired. Look upon them with the eyes of your mercy; comfort them with a sense of your goodness; preserve them from the temptations of their addiction; and give them patience under their affliction. In your time, restore them to the Program and physical, mental, and spiritual health. And help them, we pray, to listen, believe, and do your will. Amen. [39]

Blessing for Those Who Are Addicted

The Church has provided a special blessing for those who are addicted, which appears in the *Book of Blessings*, prepared by the International Commission on English in the Liturgy. The blessing can be accessed at the link provided in the Notes section.[40]

This beautiful blessing, which includes Scripture readings, is intended to strengthen the addicted person in the struggle to overcome addiction and also to assist his or her family and friends. It may be conducted by a priest, deacon, or layperson and can be repeated when pastorally appropriate.

Resources

For Alcohol and Substance Abuse

National Catholic Council on Addictions
The main objective of this organization is to offer education and spirituality resources to addicted persons and their loved ones.
  nccatoday.org/
  (800) 626-6910, ext. 1200
  E-mail: ncca@guesthouse.org

The 12-Step Review
The 12-Step Review is a publication of the Western Dominican Province, a nonprofit organization of the Dominican Fathers and Brothers, and is edited by Fr. Emmerich Vogt, OP.
  www.12-step-review.org
  (800) 556-6177

Sober Catholic
Sober Catholic is a website that discusses "how the Catholic Church, with her rich traditions of saints and miracles and especially with her sacraments such as the Holy Eucharist and Confession, can help you maintain your sobriety."
  www.sobercatholic.com
  sobercatholic@gmail.com

For Pornography/Sexual Addiction

Integrity Restored
The mission of Integrity Restored, according to its website, "is to help restore the integrity of individuals, spouses, and families that have been affected by pornography and pornography addiction. Integrity Restored provides education, encouragement, and resources to break free from pornography, heal relationships, and assist parents in preventing and responding to pornography exposure which is so devastating in the lives of our children." There is an extensive list of Catholic resources on this website that deal with pornography addiction.
www.integrityrestored.com
E-mail: admin@integrityrestored.com

Catholic Support Group for Sexual Addiction Recovery
"A Catholic group of fellow sufferers from addiction to pornography, lust, and sins of the flesh."
www.saint-mike.org/csgsar/

RECLAiM Sexual Health
RECLAiM Sexual Health offers a science-based Catholic online recovery program and other resources for those who desire to reclaim God's plan for their lives and the lives of loved ones impacted by pornography or other unhealthy sexual behaviors.
http://reclaimsexualhealth.com

Other Resources

Gam-Anon provides help for family and friends of problem gamblers.
www.gam-anon.org
(718) 352-1671
E-mail: gamanonoffice@gam-anon.org

Nar-Anon: Nar-Anon Family Groups "is primarily for those who know or have known a feeling of desperation concerning the addiction problem of someone very near to you."
www.nar-anon.org
(800) 477-6291

Al-Anon and **Alateen** provide "strength and hope for friends and families of problem drinkers."
www.al-anon.org
(757) 563-1600

The Institute of Marital Healing
"Through a combination of online resources, educational programs and publications, the Institute employs a time-tested approach to marital therapy that recognizes the importance of both science and faith in the process of marital healing."
www.maritalhealing.com
(610) 397-0950

Catholic Therapists offers referrals to professionally qualified psychotherapists who incorporate the teachings of Roman Catholicism into their practice.
www.catholictherapists.com
contactus@catholictherapists.com

Pastoral Solutions Institute is dedicated to providing the resources religiously committed Catholics need to live more faithful and abundant marriage, family, and personal lives.
www.catholiccounselors.com
(740) 266-6461
www.catholiccounselors.com

Bibliography

Beattie, Melody. *Codependent No More: How to Stop Controlling Others and Start Caring for Yourself.* Center City, MN: Hazeldon, 1992.

Carmichael, Amy. *Gold Cord: The Story of a Fellowship.* Fort Washington, PA: The Dohnavur Fellowship, 2013.

Catechism of the Catholic Church. New York: Bantam Doubleday Dell Publishing Group, 1994.

Cloud, Henry and John Townsend. *Boundaries: How to Say Yes, How to Say No to Take Control of Your Life.* Grand Rapids, MI: Zondervan Publishing House, 1992.

de Caussade, Jean-Pierre. *Abandonment to Divine Providence*, John Beevers, trans. New York: Image Books, 1975.

Degnan, Bill and Anne. *Healing Relationships.* Phoenix, AZ: Tau Publishing, 2013.

P., Bill and Lisa D. *The 12 Step Prayer Book.* Center City, MN: Hazelden, 2004.

Thérèse of Lisieux. Clarke, John, OCD, trans. *Story of a Soul: The Autobiography of St. Thérèse of Lisieux,* Washington, DC: ICS Publications, 1976.

Van Kaam, Adrian. *Personality Fulfillment in the Spiritual Life.* Wilkes-Barre, PA: Dimension Books, 1966.

VanVonderen, Jeff. *Good News for the Chemically Dependent and Those Who Love Them.* Minneapolis, MN: Bethany House, 2004.

Winkler, Jude, OFM Conv. *Daily Meditations with the Holy Spirit.* Totowa, NJ: Catholic Book Publishing Corp., 2008.

Notes

1. Project Know: Understanding Addiction, accessed at http://www.projectknow.com/research/drug-addiction-statistics-alcoholism-statistics/.

2. "Statistics on Pornography, Sexual Addiction and Online Perpetrators," Safe Families: Keeping Children Safe Online, accessed at http://www.safefamilies.org/sfStats.php.

3. "5 Alarming Gambling Addition Statistics," Addictions.com, accessed at http://www.addictions.com/. gambling/5-alarming-gambling-addiction-statistics/.

4. "Popping Pills: Prescription Drug Abuse in America," National Institute on Drug Abuse, accessed at http://www.drugabuse.gov/related-topics/trends-statistics/infographics/popping-pills-prescription-drug-abuse-in-america.

5. "Addiction and Rehab Therapy Statistics Resource Guide," GoMentor.com, accessed at http://www.gomentor.com/articles/addiction-rehab-statistics.aspx.

6. Adrian Van Kaam, *Personality Fulfillment in the Spiritual Life* (Wilkes-Barre, PA: Dimension Books, 1966), p. 131.

7. Amy Carmichael, *Gold Cord: The Story of a Fellowship* (Fort Washington, PA: The Dohnavur Fellowship, 2013), p. 15.

8. Taken from the definition of "quietude," accessed at www.vocabulary.com.

9. Melody Beattie, *Codependent No More: How to Stop Controlling Others and Start Caring for Yourself* (Center City, MN: Hazelden, 1992), p. 34.

10. Howard Markel, "The D.S.M. Gets Addiction Right," *The New York Times*, June 5, 2012, accessed at http://www.nytimes.com/2012/06/06/opinion/the-dsm-gets-addiction-right.html?_r=0.

11. Henry Cloud and John Townsend, *Boundaries: When to Say Yes, How to Say No to Take Control of Your Life* (Grand Rapids, MI: Zondervan Publishing House, 1992), p. 258.

12. Pope Francis, General Audience, April 9, 2014, accessed at http://w2.vatican.va/content/francesco/en/audiences/2014/documents/papa-francesco_20140409_udienza-generale.html.

13. Adapted from "Fountain of Mercy" by Barbara Kralis, Catholic Online, accessed at http://www.catholic.org/featured/headline.php?ID=1357: "A moral virtue that prompts its owner to have compassion for and to succour those in spiritual or temporal want."

14. *Catholic Household Blessings and Prayers*, ed. Bishop's Committee on the Liturgy, United States Conference of Catholic Bishops (New York: Random House, 2007), p. 48.

15. Bill P. and Lisa D., *The 12 Step Prayer Book* (Center City, MN: Hazelden, 2004), p. 5. Used with permission.

16. Letter of St. Thérèse of Lisieux to her sister Celine, dated April 25, 1893. *Letters of St. Thérèse of Lisieux*, trans. John Clarke, OCD, Volume II, 1890–1897 (Washington, DC: ICS Publications, 1988), p. 785.

17. Thérèse of Lisieux, *Story of a Soul*, trans. John Clarke (Washington, DC: ICS Publications, 1976), p. 238.

18. Jean-Pierre de Caussade, *Abandonment to Divine Providence*, trans. John Beevers (New York: Image Books, 1975), p. 20.

19. Ibid., pp. 108, 110.

20. Ibid., p. 114.

21. "Pope: Sad Christian Faces Are Like Pickled Peppers," May 10, 2013, accessed at http://www.catholicnewsagency.com/news/pope-sad-christian-faces-are-like-pickled-peppers/.

22. "Revelations of Our Lord to St. Margaret Mary Alacoque," Heart to Heart: A Mission to Encourage Personal Devotion to the Sacred Heart of Jesus, accessed at http://sacredheartdevotion.com/.

23. Ibid.

24. "The Dark Years," The Dublin Diocesan Matt Talbot website, accessed at http://www.matttalbot.ie/dark-years.htm.

25. Bill and Anne Degnan, *Healing Relationships* (Phoenix, AZ: Tau Publishing, 2013), p. 61. Used by permission of Vesuvius Press Inc., 4806 S. 40th St., Phoenix, AZ.

26. Thérèse of Lisieux, "Counsels and Reminiscences," *Soeur Thérèse, The Little Flower of Jesus*, ed. T. N. Taylor (London: Burns, Oates & Washbourne, 1912). Accessed at Christian Classics Ethereal Library, http://www.ccel.org/ccel/therese/autobio.xxi.html.

27. Jeff VanVonderen, *Good News for the Chemically Dependent and Those Who Love Them* (Minneapolis, MN: Bethany House, 2004), p. 120.

28. "Pope Francis to Addicts: 'You Are Never Alone,'" accessed at https://www.osv.com/OSVNewsweekly/InFocus/Article/TabId/721/ArtMID/13629/ArticleID/17163/Pope-Francis-to-addicts-%E2%80%98You-are-never-alone%E2%80%99.aspx.

29. Jude Winkler, OFM Conv, *Daily Meditations with the Holy Spirit* (Totowa, NJ: Catholic Book Publishing Corp., 2008), p. 14.

30. "How to Recite the Chaplet," The Divine Mercy, accessed at http://www.thedivinemercy.org/message/devotions/praythechaplet.php.

31. Adapted from "A Novena to Matt Talbot for Alcoholics," Venerable Matt Talbot Resource Center, accessed at http://venerablematttalbotresourcecenter.blogspot.com/2008/05/novena-to-matt-talbot-for-alcoholics.html.

32. Adapted from "St. Monica, Patron of Married Women and Mothers," Catholic Fire, accessed at http://catholicfire.blogspot.com/2008/08/st-monica-patron-of-married-women-and.html.

33. "St. Monica Novena," Pray More Novenas, accessed at http://www.praymorenovenas.com/st-monica-novena/#ixzz3s4DLZIKo.

34. "Prayer to Maximilian Maria Kolbe for Families and Friends of Someone Addicted to Drugs," accessed at http://catholicphil.tripod.com/addict.htm.

35. "St. Jude Prayer for Addiction," The National Shrine of St. Jude blog, accessed at http://blog.shrineofstjude.org/post/st-jude-prayer-for-addiction/.

36. "A Prayer to Sts. Michael, Gabriel and Raphael, Archangels," Catholic Doors Ministry, accessed at http://www.catholicdoors.com/prayers/english4/p02940.htm.

37. Adapted from a prayer found at "Prayers for Purity," Our Catholic Prayers, accessed at http://www.ourcatholicprayers.com/prayers-for-purity.html.

38. *Handbook of Devotion to the Divine Mercy* (Stockbridge, MA: Marian Press, 1996), p. 74.

39. Bill P. and Lisa D., *The 12 Step Prayer Book* (Center City, MN: Hazelden, 2004), p. 21. Used with permission.

40. *Book of Blessings*, prepared by the International Commission on English in the Liturgy: A Joint Commission of Catholic Bishops' Conferences (Collegeville, MN: The Liturgical Press, 1989). Accessed at www.catholicculture.org/culture/liturgicalyear/prayers/view.cfm?id=716.

41. From Survival to Recovery (Virginia Beach, VA : Al-Anon Family Groups Inc., 1994), p. 201.

the WORD
among us®
The *Spirit* of Catholic Living

This book was published by The Word Among Us. Since 1981, The Word Among Us has been answering the call of the Second Vatican Council to help Catholic laypeople encounter Christ in the Scriptures.

The name of our company comes from the prologue to the Gospel of John and reflects the vision and purpose of all of our publications: to be an instrument of the Spirit, whose desire is to manifest Jesus' presence in and to the children of God. In this way, we hope to contribute to the Church's ongoing mission of proclaiming the gospel to the world so that all people would know the love and mercy of our Lord and grow more deeply in their faith as missionary disciples.

Our monthly devotional magazine, *The Word Among Us*, features meditations on the daily and Sunday Mass readings, and currently reaches more than one million Catholics in North America and another half million Catholics in one hundred countries around the world. Our book division, The Word Among Us Press, publishes numerous books, Bible studies, and pamphlets that help Catholics grow in their faith.

To learn more about who we are and what we publish, log on to our website at www.wau.org. There you will find a variety of Catholic resources that will help you grow in your faith.

Embrace His Word, Listen to God . . .

www.wau.org